The Lord
Is with Thee

Hervé Aubin, OMI

The Lord Is with Thee

Notre-Dame du Cap — Novalis

The Lord Is with Thee is the English version of *Le Seigneur est avec Toi*

Translation and adaptation: Raymond ven der Buhs for Novalis, Saint Paul University, Ottawa

Photography: Gordon Shehyn (Rose-Anne Monna sculptures)

Design and Layout: Helvetigraf Inc., Québec

Sanctuaire Notre-Dame du Cap,
622, rue Notre-Dame,
Cap-de-la-Madeleine, Québec G8T 4G9

Novalis,
(375 Rideau Street),
P. O. Box 9700, Terminal,
Ottawa, Ontario K1G 4B4

ISBN 2-921012-03-0 (Notre-Dame du Cap,)
ISBN 2-89088-362-0 (Novalis)

Printed in Canada

TABLE OF CONTENTS

Part Two

SHE IS ALSO OUR MOTHER

* * *

FOREWORD

A new era of Marian devotion has resulted from the inspired direction given by the Second Vatican Council concerning our blessed mother. Above all, she is the most holy mother of God, the "Theotokos" so dearly honoured by the early Christians. She is also mother of the Church and a model of faith for those who have chosen to side with Christ. In the world and the Church of today, she is a shining sign of hope in the coming of God's kingdom. A pre-eminent member of the communion of saints, she is a most powerful advocate for all the people of God, "full of grace, fountain of beauty, model of virtue."

The Council emphasized Mary's two fundamental roles and her two essential titles: mother of God and mother of the Church. Basically, as Christians, we like to know what these say about the Blessed Virgin, about the Church and about our own personal involvement in the mystery of grace of both Mary and the Church.

We must be most grateful to Father Hervé Aubin, OMI, who accepted the challenge of presenting the Church's teaching on Mary in simple, straightforward language. His words flow from the Scriptures and from the depth of his heart. The authour is a priest of deep faith and loving dedication to our Lady. He painstakingly heeds the Council's caution to "avoid the falsity of exaggeration on the one hand, and the excess of narrow-mindedness on the other.'' The result is a sensitive and balanced — but passionately faithful — account of the importance of Mary in our lives.

Father Aubin's book is a remarkable tribute to Pope John Paul II's encyclical *Redemptoris Mater* (mother of the Redeemer), and his grace-filled gift to the people of God, the 1987-1988 Marian Year. Our Holy Father wrote: ''The Marian Year is meant to promote a new and more careful reading of what the Council said about the Blessed Virgin Mary, mother of God, in the Mystery of Christ and the Church.''

Father Aubin has made a magnificent contribution in that regard. May the Lord be with him for his efforts, and may ''the Lord be with thee'' as you read this book.

Louis-Albert Vachon
Archbishop of Québec
Primate of Canada
March, 1988

INTRODUCTION

A Beautiful Experience

One March morning, near the small shrine of Notre-Dame du Cap, a station wagon came to a stop. A woman with a bundle in her arms sat in the front. From the back of the car, three or four young children watched their father as he walked towards me. He was about thirty-five years old. "Is the small shrine open? We've just left the hospital with our new-born daughter. We want to show her the Blessed Virgin Mary as early in her life as possible."

I found this experience so beautiful! I was thinking of them when I wrote this book. I thought of their family and of their little girl, who must be nine or ten years old now. This book is for them and for those who love the Virgin Mary, who want to know more about her and who want to learn from their "mother" how to grow in life as children of God.

No Cosmetics Needed

As Christians, we believe in Jesus and his word. Our main guide is the Bible which comes to us through the Church. This is true not only as regards Jesus, but as regards his mother Mary as well.

You've no doubt heard a lot of talk about Mary. Some people do not accept the teachings of the Gospels about her. They refuse to believe that Mary became the mother of Jesus while remaining a virgin. Others scorn us for praying to her. They accuse us of placing Mary on an equal footing with God! And there are some who indulge in exaggeration when speaking of the mother of God. They latch on to the "extraordinary" and make that the basis for their devotion.

Mary is beautiful as is! God made her that way. God worked wonders in her. What could our "cosmetics" add to the one among us who is the most like God?

Mary: Mother, Sister and Disciple

This book is not a ''life'' of the Virgin Mary. The Gospels, which are our source of information, do not provide biographical data on Jesus, or on his mother. They give us facts which are important to our faith, but they do not give us the kinds of details we would expect to find in a biography.

However, after reflecting on Scripture, it is amazing how much we can discover about Mary! This is what the Church did at Vatican II, and we are going to do the same. By doing this, we will, like John, the beloved disciple to whom Jesus gave his mother, and like the millions of disciples who revere Mary, take her ''into our home.''

Let us unite with John Paul II, Saint Theresa of the Child Jesus, Mother Teresa, our ancestors of long ago, as well as those of recent times, and all who have found in Mary the strength and courage to remain faithful.

Together we will learn what God has done for Mary. We will call her ''blessed'' and say of her: ''The Lord is with thee!'' We will show our love for her and venerate her for what she is: the mother of our Lord Jesus Christ and his first disciple. She is our mother and also our sister in the family of God.

Part One

MARY: THE MOTHER OF JESUS AND HIS FIRST DISCIPLE

Hail, Mary, full of grace,
the Lord is with thee.
Blessed art thou amongst women
and blessed is the fruit of thy womb, Jesus.

Chapter 1

Growing up Jewish

Mary was a Jewish woman, raised in the religion of her people. She knew what God had done for Israel. She learned that God chose Israel, despite its small number of people. God took care of the people, protected them, and made an alliance with them.

From the Bible Mary discovered that her people were not always faithful, but that God did not change and kept the promise to help those who trusted him. People of good will understood this and, in spite of evil times, remained steadfast in their faith. They said to themselves: "God will not abandon us. God will not allow us to fall." Mary's family came from people such as these.

God's Chosen People

At home and in the synagogue, Mary learned what had happened to her people in the past. She saw how good God had been to them.

Who was Mary? She was a Jewish woman and she belonged to the people with whom the Lord had chosen to make a covenant. At an early age, she understood that God had "intentionally" chosen Israel, which was an insignificant nation in terms of power and numbers. Mary's people were no better than others, and they did not merit this favour. It was out of love—and freely — that God had chosen them.

God had promised to look after and to help the Jewish people. God offered to make an agreement with them, a covenant. It was a commitment under oath. If the people trusted God, God would always be there and would never let them fall. Many times the Lord freed them from rich and powerful nations. Above all, everyone remembered the liberation from slavery in Egypt. Each year people celebrated this great intervention by God which was called Easter and which signified the "passover" of the Lord.

Mary's people were no better than others. It was out of love — and freely — that God had chosen them.

No one could forget what had taken place. During the celebrations they recalled what God had done for them. As a child, Mary heard about her ancestors and their extraordinary faith and hope. First, there was Abraham, the father of all believers. Without knowing what the consequences would be, he answered "yes" to the Lord. "He was convinced that God had power to do what he had promised" (Romans 4:21). There was also Moses, the great prophet, who guided the people out of Egypt and through the desert. And, of course, there was King David. God had promised that one of his descendants would reign on his throne forever.

God Remained Faithful

God does not hold a grudge. The chosen people abandoned God many times, but because of love for them, God always remained faithful.

The Bible does not conceal anything. The young Mary learned that her people had not always been faithful to God. At times they were tempted to embrace the gods of the pagan religions. Often also, when faced with the menacing presence of powerful neighbouring countries, they became afraid. They even doubted that God was capable of protecting them. Because of their lack of faith, God left the Hebrews to their own weaknesses. They lost their wars and found themselves in exile in enemy territory.

Nevertheless, even in these difficult times, God did not abandon the chosen people. God raised up prophets in their midst to inspire trust and loyalty. Happiness and life would be theirs, the prophets patiently told the people, if only they would again trust in and be faithful to God.

Some, of course, did remain faithful in spite of the difficulties and national humiliations. They knew that God still loved them and would not forsake them.

And who were these faithful ones? The Bible says they are poor, humble, and just in their hearts — those who turned to the Lord and followed the divine will. Their refuge was the name of the Lord (See Zephaniah 2:3). These "humble of the earth" formed the small "remnant of Israel" of whom the prophets speak. Without losing confidence, they trusted God's promise and awaited the "consolation of Israel." Luke speaks of them in his Gospel.

Happiness and life would be theirs, the prophets patiently told the people, if only they would again trust in and be faithful to God.

Awaiting the Promised Messiah

When Mary was growing up, people often spoke of the coming of the Messiah. They did not always understand God's promise, but everyone was eager to see it fulfilled.

Mary grew up in a "humbled" land. Palestine had been conquered by the Romans, which meant that the people of God were governed by pagans. This was a severe blow to the faith of the believers. And to make matters worses, the prophets had not spoken for a long time. There was only silence from God. In spite of all this, the people remembered God's promise and continued to hope for divine intervention. They awaited the promised Messiah.

Many thought that the Messiah would be a king, a new David, who would send the Romans packing. Others were hoping for more than a simple political liberation. They awaited a Messiah who would come to fulfill God's promises of happiness and life.

The people had many questions. They asked: "When will the Messiah come?" and "How will we recognize the Messiah?" There weren't any simple answers, but the people continued to wait and hope.

Mary's Vocation

A little girl, called Mary, was chosen by God to be the mother of the Messiah, for whom all the world was waiting.

The time was approaching when God would fulfill the hopes of the poor. From among them, the Lord had chosen a little girl. She was called Mary, or Miriam in the language of her country. God had chosen her to accomplish "great things."

No one, even Mary herself, knew that she was different from anyone else. Not until later, at the Annunciation, did she learn that God had looked on her in a special way. God had chosen her, Mary of Nazareth, from among all the others to be the mother of the Messiah, whom God had promised for hundreds and hundreds of years. This was the day that Abraham had hoped to see.

The Bible does not speak of Mary's parents. But an apocryphal (this term is explained in the boxed note which follows) text identifies them as Joachim and Anne. This text tells us about Mary's birth in much the same way that the Gospels recount the birth of Christ. For example, we are told that an angel announced to Joachim that he would have a daughter called Mary. Anne, who was sterile according to this text, would miraculously become pregnant. However, we have no reason to believe that Mary was miraculously born. The Bible does not state this, nor has the Church ever taught this. Mary was born of the conjugal union of her parents, as all of us are.

Artists often depict St. Anne with Mary. The mother holds an open book which she is showing to her little girl. This reminds us that Mary's mother was the first to teach her the history of her people. It was St. Anne who first talked to Mary about "the one who was to come."

God chose Mary of Nazareth to accomplish "great things."

THE ''APOCRYPHAL'' WRITINGS

When we call something ''apocryphal,'' we mean that it is a text which the Church does not recognize as part of the Bible — a book not inspired by the Holy Spirit, as are the other biblical writings. The apocrypha attempt to show the greatness of Mary and Jesus, but are often written in a naive way and sometimes even in bad taste. While the Gospels give few details on the lives of Jesus and Mary, the apocrypha will recount their lives with all sorts of exaggerations and ''facts.'' The intention to show the greatness of Jesus and his mother was a good one, but the manner was debatable. In short: we should not take everything written in the apocrypha as the ''word of the Gospel.''

The best known of these writings is the Protogospel of James. The first part of the book was written about a hundred years after the death of Jesus, but the entire book, as we know it today, could be dated in the fifth century.

According to these apocryphal writings, Mary was presented in the Temple of Jerusalem at the age of three and lived there until the age of twelve. This is quite impossible since there was no place in the Temple where little girls could live. Basically, what the apocryphal writings wish to teach is that the child Mary was already living for her God and walking in the divine presence. This is perfectly correct.

The young Mary's only desire was to consecrate herself to the Lord, to be God's servant and to love God with all her heart. In other words, she sought to live fully the Jewish faith that she professed each day: "Listen Israel: Yahweh our God is the one Yahweh. You shall love Yahweh your God with all your heart, with all your soul, with all your strength..." (Deuteronomy 6:4-5).

Looking to the Future

Mary pondered in her heart what God had said and done for the chosen people. How she longed for the promise to be fulfilled and for God to come at last and visit among them!

With the ''humble'' people, Mary meditated and pondered the words and actions of Yahweh. With all her heart, she wished that the day would come when God's promises would be fulfilled. How she desired the coming of the one on whom '' the spirit of Yahweh rests... He does not judge by appearances, he gives no verdict on hearsay, but judges the wretched with integrity and, with equity, gives a verdict for the poor of the land'' (Isaiah 11:2-4).

Mary stands out among the poor and humble ...who confidently await and receive salvation from the Lord.

***Lumen Gentium**, No. 55*

Chapter 2

Filled with God's Favour

God wants us to be holy: living and happy in the divine presence. This is why God created us.

But Adam and Eve did not believe, and the human race cut itself off from the source of life and happiness. As a result, we are born into a world that has turned its back on God. We call this original sin. Fortunately, God has not abandoned us to our folly. God's Son came to restore us and fill us with divine life.

The first one to be filled with the love of the Lord was Mary. From the moment of her conception she was holy and immaculate.

In the Beginning...

Though created to find our life and our happiness in God, we chose to look elsewhere, and that was our error.

In the beginning, man and woman were created to be intimate with God, to be God's friends.

We know what happened. Our first ancestors, Adam and Eve, did not trust in God. They decided that they could live on their own, without God. By living their life in their own way, they distanced themselves from God. The consequences were tragic. This human arrogance changed our character and changed the world. We no longer have a natural inclination toward God, and egoism and deceit often deform our relations with our fellow human beings.

Original sin is "this separation from God, which touches all people at their birth, and leaves in their hearts a tendency to distrust, to lie, to disobey, to revolt, to break away from God who has never stopped loving us."

John Paul II, at Lourdes,
August 14, 1983.

How did God react? Fortunately, God did not simply leave us and say: "Take care of everything by yourself, since that is what you want to do in your arrogance!" Rather we are invited to return, to once again be God's friends and God's children. We chose to separate ourselves from God, and only God can "rebuild the bridges."

On our own, we remain on the outside where we put ourselves. Alone, we can only be distant from God. Children come into the world deprived of "parentage" with God. This is what we call original sin.

God Continues to Love Us

God did not become discouraged by the sin of the human race. To each person is offered the possibility of becoming God's child and sharing in divine life.

In spite of original sin, God loves new-born children. There can be no doubt about this since God is love and God loves the whole world. God loves us from beginning to end. God loves an unborn baby that is still no more than a fetus, no more than an embryo, just as he loves an older person dying of old age. We were still in our mother's wombs when God looked on us with love. We are created in the divine image and likeness. This, however, does not obscure the fact that we all share one thing in common that is far from beautiful: we have separated ourselves from God from the beginning.

How is God going to return humanity to the life that it has discarded? God always invites us to share in the divine life, and each of us will have the occasion to personally respond to this invitation. For us, this begins with baptism. The Lord has given us rebirth into a new life. We receive this life by the death and resurrection of Jesus.

At our baptism, we became God's children. At the same time, we joined the family of God's Son. We became members of the Church. From that moment on, with divine help, we can live our life in the "friendship" of God.

What about those who are not baptized? The Council reminds us that God also gathers in, through the Spirit of the risen Christ, those who do not know God. For "God wants everyone to be saved and reach full knowledge of the truth" (1 Timothy 2:4).

How Mary helps us... to accept the word and love of God with an open heart and to believe in spite of the doubts that our society and our own spirit harbour!

John Paul II, in Lourdes, August 15, 1983.

What about Mary?

God loved Mary in a special way and so preserved her from all stain of sin.

People are sometimes surprised to hear that Mary has been redeemed and that she is the "first person to be saved." They say: "The Blessed Virgin never sinned. She had no need to be saved." They are correct in asserting that Mary never sinned. She was faithful to God with all her heart. From the time she was a small child to the end of her life, she never hesitated to follow God. In this way Mary is different from us, because we do not always live in the light of God. Sometimes we try not to hear God's call. But even when we do hear, we do not always have the strength and generosity to respond. Mary did not go through this humiliating experience.

Mary is truly a human being and, like us, she is a daughter of Adam; she has been redeemed, like us, by the blood of the Lamb; the grace which has filled her is, as with us, the grace of adoption.

The Quebec Bishops,
***The Virgin Mary in Christian Life in Quebec Today**, No. 13.*

How is this possible? Was not Mary human like the rest of us? Certainly Mary is our earthly sister. Like us, she descends from the first ancestors who separated themselves from their Creator. If God had not intervened to fill her with divine life from the beginning of her existence, she would have lacked the life of grace just as we do when we come into the world. But God had favoured her from the moment of her conception. So that she could be worthy of being the mother of the Saviour, God kept her free from all stain of sin.

Created in a State of Grace

A mother, holy and pure, was what God wanted for the Son. From the beginning of her existence in the womb of her mother, Mary was filled with the favour of God.

Some people believe that the Immaculate Conception is the way in which Mary conceived Jesus, through an action of the Holy Spirit. This is not correct. The Immaculate Conception means that from the beginning of her existence in her mother's womb, Mary was united with God. Before entering into the world she was filled with God's favour.

The future mother of the Saviour was conceived as any other human child, by the loving union of a father and mother. Her soul, however, was created in a state of grace, filled with the love of God, preserved from sin and saved in advance from sin. This was a gift of grace. God is absolutely free with divine gifts.

Everything done for this child, was done freely. Mary was honoured to admit that everything came to her from God. She sang this clearly in the Magnificat: "He has looked upon his lowly handmaid... the Almighty has done great things for me. Holy is his name..." (Luke 1:48-49).

Let us remember that God "loved us first" (1 John 4:19). God freely took us into the family and freely extended to us divine friendship. This is what we call the state of grace. This same life "flows" in us as in Mary. In us it began at baptism, but in Mary it started from the moment of her conception.

THE IMMACULATE CONCEPTION BECOMES PART OF THE CATHOLIC FAITH

Pope Pius IX solemnly defined this doctrine on December 8, 1854:

"We declare and pronounce and define that the doctrine which holds that the Blessed Virgin Mary, in the first instant of her conception, has been, by a grace and privilege of almighty God, and in view of the merits of Jesus Christ, Saviour of the human race, preserved and exempted from every stain of original sin, is revealed by God, and consequently is to be believed firmly and inviolably by all the faithful."

Ineffabilis Deus, No. 47.

This life is given to Mary — and to us — by the grace of Jesus Christ. In view of the merits of the Son, God made the Blessed Virgin holy in her mother's womb. Jesus is the Saviour of everyone, "the bridge" between God and us. Everything happens through Jesus — there are no exceptions. Even Mary, his mother, was saved through her Son.

The grace of being a child of God is one which only Jesus, the beloved Child of the Father, can give. For us, as for Mary, "something of God" has been given and something of God has begun within us. This something is so strong that it will overcome death and last for eternity.

What we are carrying around in our fragile bodies is the treasure of the life of God. Mary was filled with this from the first instant of her existence.

The grace that others receive with baptism, God gave to Mary even before her birth, in view of the merits of Christ, in order to prepare her to be the mother of the Saviour.

The U.S. Bishops,
***Behold Your Mother**, No. 53.*

Chapter 3

You Will Have a Son

God ''in person'' will come into our world. God will ask Mary of Nazareth for a human life. In the name of all humanity, the young woman welcomed the Saviour that God gave us. Freely, she cooperated with the plan of God to save us.

Jesus will not have a human father. His Father is God. Therefore, it is from God that he comes to us. And it is God's choice that he come to us. Since we could not give ourselves a Saviour, he had to come from God.

Your faith gave us
The one foretold
By people of hope.
Joy of prophets
God formed in your body
The eternal image
Who became one of us.

(Sr. Marie-Pierre)

God Proposes Respectfully

It is through a woman that the Son of God came into our world. He became one of us to comfort us "not as a stranger, but as a brother" (Laurentin).

What would we have suggested if God had said to us: "Choose the manner in which I should come to save you"? Never would we have dared to respond: "Be one of us. Be a human being." We would never have thought of such a thing, because it is such a staggering idea. Just imagine, the Creator of the universe becoming one of us! God, thrice Holy, taking on our human limitations! Truly, only God could have thought of such a thing!

For the Creator of the world, the greatest and most beautiful way to come into the world was through a woman: to be formed and carried in her womb, nourished with her milk, cradled with her tenderness and taught by her to walk and to speak.

This woman is the one who always recalls the love of God to a world that ignores this love or no longer wishes to believe in it. It is she who reminds us that God gave us his only Son, the Word, that he became a human being in her and by her, and that he lived among us.

John Paul II, at Lourdes,
August 15, 1983.

God did not want to impose upon us in becoming a human being; rather God "proposed." In a delicate way and with respect for our liberty, God wished to have our response before becoming incarnate. Mary of Nazareth would be asked to welcome God in our name. The divine decision to come into our world was to depend upon the consent of this young woman. Our salvation would also depend on it.

Mary Responds Freely

Mary freely became the mother of Jesus, and not by surprise or force as some people would have us believe. God always respects human freedom.

Some people who do not know the gospel account of the Annunciation or who have not learned it properly, suggest that Mary became pregnant "by surprise." They speak as if she had been forced, "violated" by God. But if we read Luke 1:26-38 carefully, we see very clearly that Mary was given a chance to speak before accepting what God was proposing. The Gospel of Luke portrays a young woman who dialogues with a messenger of God. She seeks clarification before giving her response.

God does not impose salvation. Nor did God impose it on Mary. With the Annunciation, God turned to her in a very personal manner, seeking her will and awaiting a response which came forth from her faith.

John Paul II, at Ephesus,
November 30, 1979.

When the angel Gabriel announced that she was going to be a mother, Mary asked: "But how can this come about, since I am a virgin?" Or, according to another translation, "since I do not know any man" (Luke 1:34). Does Mary want to tell us here that she had decided to remain a virgin? Most Christians think so. It seems that the Greek text (the Gospel was written in that language) would allow for other interpretations of Mary's response. Let us note, however, that the Church generally interprets these words to mean that Mary had decided to remain a virgin.

One thing is clear and certain: Mary became a mother while remaining a virgin. She became pregnant because she wanted to. God proposed this maternity to her, and she freely accepted. The important point here is that before undertaking the Incarnation, the Lord waited for the consent of the young woman from Nazareth.

I Am the Servant of the Lord

Mary responded to God enthusiastically. "Yes!" she answered. It was the yes of one who loves God and who asks nothing more than to be at the service of God's loving plan for humanity.

Mary's response: Is it possible to imagine any other human undertaking that could have such a repercussion as the "yes" of this woman? The "yes" of the Annunciation is so important because it came from a human being. It made the divine coming among us dependent on a human response!

With her response, Mary involved herself completely in God's plan for our salvation. This is what she wished to affirm when she said: "I am the servant of the Lord." In the Bible, "Servant of God" is a title of honour. It refers to a person who collaborates with God.

Is it possible that Mary knew in advance what being a servant of God would imply? No, Mary did not know what was to come. However, she knew the most important thing: that "nothing is impossible to God." She knew that God was there, with her, helping accomplish the task with which she had been entrusted. With faith and generosity, Mary answered "yes" to God. She gave her word and stood by it: "I am the handmaid of the Lord, let what you have said be done to me" (Luke 1:38).

MARY'S JOYFUL "YES"

Mary's joyful "yes" witnesses to her internal liberty, confidence and serenity. She did not know how her service to the Lord would unfold, nor what the life of her Son would be. But this did not create in her fear and anguish. Rather, she remained totally free and open. "Behold the servant of the Lord." It was God's will that would be her light in life, her peace in suffering and her joy.

John Paul II, in Switzerland,
June 17, 1984.

And the unbelievable happened! In a very remote part of the world, in a little, insignificant village, a young woman carried in her the thrice Holy God! No one else knows but the young mother! God is there — a small, human embryo in her body.

Pregnant without Conjugal Relations

Mary became pregnant with Jesus while remaining a virgin and without having relations with Joseph. She gave birth to the Saviour through the power of the Holy Spirit.

Some people ridicule this fact, while others simply do not believe. True believers speak with respect of the "marvels" that God has realized in Mary. They do not forget what is said in the *Creed* about Jesus Christ, our Lord: he "was conceived by the Holy Spirit; born of the Virgin Mary." Jesus was born of a virgin mother. The Church has always considered this to be true.

From the beginning, Christians believed that Mary, the mother of Jesus, became pregnant through the action of the Holy Spirit. We can find this in Gabriel's announcement to Mary (Luke 1:34-35) and also in an angel's announcement to Joseph (Matthew 1:18).

Mary and Joseph had to keep the virginal conception a secret for a long time. Why? Because their neighbours would not have understood. Imagine the reaction of the inhabitants of Nazareth if Mary had said: "I had my little boy directly through the power of God without having relations with Joseph."

People would have been uncomfortable with this, and some would have laughed. Others would have made coarse jokes. Even today we hear trite remarks from some baptized Catholics. No, Mary could not talk about it since it would have been like "throwing pearls before swine.'' Not until much later, after the Resurrection of Jesus, could she speak about it. By that time the Spirit of Pentecost had enlightened the disciples.

The Holy Spirit helped the disciples to undertand that the Son of Mary was truly the Son of God, and that he was God. Mary was now free to speak, and she could take the disciples into her confidence. She could share the secret that she had carried within herself for more than thirty years.

The Spirit, who had already infused the fullness of grace into Mary of Nazareth, formed the human nature of Christ in her virginal womb.

John Paul II,
Redemptoris Mater, No. 1.

Only God Can Save Us

Jesus is born of a virgin and not of the union of a man and a woman. Why? Because God wants us to understand that we could not, on our own, give ourselves a Saviour. Salvation is a gift of God.

Why was the Lord born of a virgin? What does God want to tell us by this marvel? One thing is certain, God does not wish to discredit the union of man and woman. God made human love and said: "Be fruitful, multiply..." (Genesis 1:28). God's work cannot be negated or undone.

By having the Son born of a virgin woman, God wished to tell us two things. Firstly, Jesus is the Son of God. By coming into the world without the intervention of a human father, God wants to show us that the Son has only one Father: his heavenly Father. Secondly, we cannot, on our own, give ourselves a Saviour. Look at the closest couple that you know. They cannot one day decide: "Let us have a child who will be the Saviour of the world!"

Only God can decide to save us. Neither Mary nor any other person could have done this. God took the lead. Remember this: because Jesus was born of Mary, he is truly of this world. But he also came from elsewhere, from the heavenly Father. Salvation does not come from us, but from God.

Humanity had a new start in Jesus. The conception of the Son of Mary, without a human father, is a sign that the Incarnation is the new creation, independent of the human will or of the impulse of the flesh.

The U.S. Bishops,
Behold Your Mother, No. 24.

Her Son Is God

The child that Mary carried inside her, that she brought into the world and nourished with her milk, is the Son of God in person. This is why we say that Mary is the mother of God.

Ask people if they are believers. Often the answers will be: "Yes, I believe the world did not come about by itself, but was made by a supreme Being." Or, "There is someone or something who runs everything from on high."

As you can see, these people believe in a God who made the world, and this is good. But they do not see the relationship between Jesus and this Supreme Being of whom they speak. They are believers who call themselves Christian, but they do not speak of Jesus Christ. They do not seem to know that God, who created the world, also became human through the Virgin Mary.

And yet these same people often pray to the Blessed Virgin. This is curious. They say in the *Hail Mary*: "Holy Mary, mother of God." And Mary is indeed the mother of God since the child she brought into the world is the Son of God, the second person of the Holy Trinity.

Through her child, Mary reminds us of the core of our Christian faith: the belief that God became one of us. The Word of God is part of our human flesh. This is the mystery of the Incarnation. God the Son, the Word of the Father, became a human being through Mary.

You ask me if I am a believer. I answer, yes, I am a believer, I am a Christian.

I know and I believe that the Creator of the world is my heavenly Father. I know and I believe that his Son became human through the Holy Spirit, that he was born of the Virgin Mary, that he is the Saviour of the world, and that he has made me a child of God.

In short: being a Christian means knowing and believing that Mary brought into the world the one through whom "all things came to be" (John 1:3).

From the moment of her pregnancy, Mary was to be mother of a child who is God. The Son of Mary was not simply a man whom God intended to adopt after the fact. Some people say this, but it is false.

The Christian faith clearly states that Jesus is truly the Son of God. Let us point out again that the Son of Mary is the same as the Son of God. He is one and the same being, and the same person.

Mary is the mother of God, "certainly not in the blasphemous sense that she existed before God, but as an affirmation of the truth of the Incarnation. The Son of Mary is the only person to be the Son of God, Emmanuel."

The U.S. Bishops,
***Behold Your Mother**, No. 63.*

Christ is God. And the Son of God is Jesus whom Mary carried and brought into the world. Jesus is simultaneously God and a human being.

Chapter 4

God Invites Us to Rejoice

God brings joy for all to share. At the Annunciation, God invited us to rejoice through the Angel Gabriel who told Mary: "Rejoice."

When Luke writes about the Annunciation, he does not mention the Virgin's reaction. When Mary visits with Elizabeth, the Gospel has her say the canticle of thanksgiving and joy that we call the *Magnificat*. (*Magnificat* is the first word of the Latin translation of this canticle which begins with Mary saying that her soul magnifies the Lord.)

A Joyous God

Joy is a word we often find in the Bible. God is joyous by nature. God announces a visit among us to bring us joy. ''Rejoice'' is the first word the Angel Gabriel says to Mary.

We are right to wish others ''Merry Christmas'' or ''Happy Easter.'' These are joyful days filled with God. God is joyful because God is life and love.

God asks us to share in the divine joy. In the Bible the people are asked to rejoice, "for the Lord is coming." We use these encouraging words in the Advent season. See how beautiful the following example is! ''Shout for joy, daughter of Zion, Israel, shout aloud! Rejoice, exult with all your heart, daughter of Jerusalem....Yahweh your God is in your midst, a victorious warrior. He will exult with joy over you, he will renew you by his love; he will dance with shouts of joy for you as on a day of festival'' (Zephaniah 3:14, 17).

You have read correctly — God will dance for us! The Old Testament is not just a religion of fear. God does sometimes ''speak strongly'' in order to educate the chosen people and to make them understand some things. At the same time we are often told not to fear, but to rejoice, *because God is coming*.

It is not surprising what the Angel Gabriel said to Mary: ''Rejoice, so highly favoured! The Lord is with you'' (Luke 1:28).

RECOGNIZING GOD WHO IS COMING

It is quite normal for a woman six months pregnant to feel the movements of the baby in her womb. But when a mother can tell that it is joy that is causing the little one to "leap," then something very special has happened. This is what happened when Mary went to visit Elizabeth. The baby leaped with joy when Mary entered Elizabeth's home and greeted her.

Filled with the Holy Spirit, Elizabeth recognized that the child Mary carried was the Lord. The Holy Spirit helps us to recognize the Lord in the one who comes to visit us. The Holy Spirit also helps us to rejoice and to welcome the Lord who comes to renew us with divine love (see Zephaniah 3:17).

Mary knew this: she recognized, in this greeting, the great invitation to the people of God to rejoice. She remembered the prophet's words, which we read earlier. This invitation to rejoice was first received by Mary. Coming to her in the most unimaginable and intimate way, God lived inside her! She received God in the name of all her people. The birth of the Messiah was to be a joy for all. The Lord came for everyone, as the angel at Bethlehem was to tell the shepherds nine months later: "I bring you news of great joy, a joy to be shared by the whole people. Today in the town of David a Saviour has been born to you" (Luke 2:10-11).

God comes to share his joy with us. Jesus will later affirm: "I have told you this so that my joy may be in you..." (John 15:11). He also told us how he would greet us on our arrival: ''Well done, good and faithful servant...come and join in your master's happiness'' (Matthew 25:21).

The God of the Bible, the God we know, is not a God of fear and sadness, but a God of joy. That is why God always invites us this way: ''Rejoice. I am with you.'' This is the same joy of God that overcame Mary and made her sing her *Magnificat.*

We learn from Mary the secret of the joy that comes from the faith, to illumine our life and that of others. The gospel account of the Visitation is filled with joy: the joy of being visited by God, the joy of opening the doors to the Redeemer. This joy is the fruit of the Holy Spirit, and no one can take it away from us, if we remain faithful to God.

John Paul II, at Notre-Dame du Cap,
September 10, 1984.

All Generations Will Call Her Blessed

God loved Mary. She opened herself to divine love and hence to God. That is why she was overflowing with joy.

Mary was happy. She saw herself as an ordinary person in the eyes of God. She was no one special, but God looked on her and did great things in her.

Mary believed in what happened, and she did not say: "I am nothing." She did not deny the miracles that happened within her, but she recognized that what she was and had, came from the Lord. For this she was happy and thankful.

Mary appreciated so much what she had become by the grace of God, that she prophesied: all generations that hear about this will call her blessed. We sometimes say: "Humility is truth." But the truth is that we have received everything from God: what we are and what we have.

Being humble and true is to act as Mary acts in the *Magnificat*: to give glory and honour to God for everything wonderful and beautiful that happens within ourselves and in our lives.

The truth is that we have received everything from God: what we are and what we have.

Mary Sings to God

God does not forget. God is mindful of past promises. God's love is for all generations. Mary rejoices because the "little ones" who have placed their hope in God have not been deceived. Those who are relying on their wealth are sent away empty-handed.

The *Magnificat* sings of God's generosity, of God's undying love for us, of God's promises that are never broken. Mary is grateful because God focusses on the whole person and not one's power or money. Perhaps you have noticed that the *Magnificat* is not a song *to* Mary, but a song *from* Mary *to* God.

When we sing Mary's *Magnificat*, we sing a song of praise to God's love and fidelity to us. With Mary and the community of disciples, we bless the Lord who is unimpressed with money and power. We bless the Lord for taking care of the little ones and the poor in spirit and for helping those who place their trust and confidence in God.

The *Magnificat* challenges society, both Mary's and our own. In Mary's time as today, the heads of nations were using their power forcefully; the strong were demonstrating their "importance"; power was determining everything; the mighty were crushing the small. God overturns all this, and Mary applauds.

For Mary, what counts above all else is truth and authenticity. This is why she praises God who has put deceit and arrogance "in their place."

THE MAGNIFICAT

My soul proclaims the greatness of the Lord, my spirit rejoices in God my Saviour; for he has looked with favour on his lowly servant.

From this day all generations will call me blessed; the Almighty has done great things for me, and holy is his Name.

He has mercy on those who fear him in every generation.

He has shown the strength of his arm, he has scattered the proud in their conceit.

He has cast down the mighty from their thrones, and has lifted up the lowly.

He has filled the hungry with good things, and the rich he has sent away empty.

He has come to the help of his servant Israel for he has remembered his promise of mercy, the promise he made to our fathers, to Abraham and his children for ever (Luke 1:46-55).

God exalts the humble. Jesus said, "Those who humble themselves will be exalted" (Matthew 23:12). Jesus humbled himself for he did not come to be served, but to serve his brothers and sisters (Matthew 20:28). This is exactly what happened: God has exalted him because he has humbled himself by being obedient to the end. This is why God raised him high and gave him a name which is above all other names (see Philippians 2:9).

Mary, his mother, did not wish to waste her life. She did not want to risk finding herself empty-handed like those who are content with their riches and have lost all hunger and thirst for the Lord.

That is why Mary was ready to learn from her son who is "gentle and humble of heart" (Matthew 11:29). It is clear that what makes Mary rejoice will also make Jesus rejoice. He praises his Father for "revealing these things to mere children" while the arrogant, in their vanity, see nothing (see Luke 10:21).

God has "revealed these things to mere children," and Mary is among them. She is first among those who know how to be humble and poor in spirit.

The modern woman will note with pleasant surprise that Mary of Nazareth, while completely devoted to the will of God, was far from being a timidly submissive woman or one whose piety was repelling to others; on the contrary, she was a woman who did not hesitate to proclaim that God vindicates the humble and the oppressed, and removes the powerful people of this world from their privileged positions (see Luke 1:51-53).

Paul VI,
***Marialis Cultus*, No. 37.**

Chapter 5

Mary and Joseph, the Couple

At Nazareth, everybody knew each other, or thought they did. In their family circle, Mary and Joseph were a couple like any other. Their neighbours simply believed that Jesus was the son of Joseph, but Mary and Joseph knew where their "treasure" came from. They both had one purpose in mind, and that was to raise Jesus in the best way they could. And "Jesus lived under their authority" (Luke 2:51).

As the bride
is to the groom
the heart of Mary
was to Joseph.

(St. John Eudes)

Engagement in the Jewish Community

Engagement in the Jewish community was more than a promise of marriage. Engaged couples were expected to be as committed to one another as were married couples.

When thinking of the engagement of Mary and Joseph, we must not forget that the customs of their country were different from ours. Engagement in Israel took place at a very young age compared to our country. The normal age for a girl was between twelve and twelve and a half years. For a boy it was between sixteen and twenty-two years. Eighteen years was considered the ideal age for his engagement.

We should repeat that in Mary and Joseph's time, engagement was more than a promise of marriage. Practically speaking, engagement was considered a commitment like that between married people. An engaged couple was often referred to as husband and wife. If one of them were to be unfaithful, he or she would be accused of adultery. In fact, sexual relations during the engagement period were frowned upon.

How did people become engaged? The young man went to the home of the father and asked for permission to marry his daughter. If the father agreed he then made the arrangements on behalf of his daughter, for she "belonged" to her father.

A daughter was not allowed to refuse a marriage arranged by her father, until she was twelve and a half years old. That's when she had reached the age of majority. The engagement was off without her consent. But even after the age of majority it was the father who decided how much money the boy had to pay for his daughter. This money would then be kept by the father. On the other hand, the father had to provide a dowry for his daughter, which was a little like an inheritance.

Once the father and his future son-in-law had agreed on the arrangements, the engagement went into effect, but the girl remained under her father's authority until the marriage.

Marriage was usually celebrated a year after the engagement so that the girl would be a little older. We know very little about the ceremony itself. What we do know is that the man, accompanied by the bridesmaids, went to look for his fiancée to bring her in procession to his house. Jesus speaks of this in the Gospel (see Matthew 25:1 ff.).

There was a great feast with singing and dancing for the family and the neighbourhood. In most cases the young couple went to live with the groom's family. For the young woman this meant living in her in-laws' home and often with her husband's brothers and sisters. Sometimes she had to live with aunts and uncles and cousins. This may not always have been easy for a young woman of fourteen or fifteen years.

Obviously, our knowledge of these Jewish customs does not tell us exactly how Mary and Joseph came to be engaged, nor at what age their engagement took place. We can only guess. Nevertheless, it's good to be familiar with the customs of the time. This helps us remember that Mary lived at a specific time and place — she was a Jew who lived according to the customs and religion of her people about two thousand years ago.

The normal age for engagement at the time of Mary and Joseph was sixteen to twenty-two years for the boy, and twelve to twelve and a half for the girl.

Joseph Adopts Jesus

Before she was living with Joseph, Mary became pregnant by the Holy Spirit. Joseph, wishing to respect the work of God, was ready to renounce his marriage with Mary. But God wanted Joseph to pass as the father of Jesus.

Mary was already engaged — given in marriage — to Joseph, when the angel Gabriel announced the birth of the Messiah (see Luke 1:27). We also read in Matthew: "His mother Mary was betrothed to Joseph; but before they came to live together she was found to be with child through the Holy Spirit" (Matthew 1:18).

What was going to happen to Joseph? His fiancée was pregnant. The child was not his, but it was the fruit of the Holy Spirit. Joseph wanted to respect what the Lord had accomplished in his fiancée. He did not wish to interfere with the work of God.

The more he thought about it, the less he could understand how the two things could go together: his marriage with Mary and God's work in her. Joseph wished to spare Mary publicity and decided to divorce her informally (Matthew 1:19). It was then that God made it clear to Joseph that his marriage with Mary was part of the divine plan.

NO FAMILY NAME

In Israel there were many women called Mary and many men called Joseph. Even the name "Jesus" was common among the Jews.

There was no family name. In order to distinguish someone, "son of so and so" was added to the first name. This is why, in order to distinguish Jesus from the others who had this name, he was called "Jesus, son of Joseph" or, by adding his place of origin, "Jesus of Nazareth."

"'Joseph, son of David, do not be afraid to take Mary home as your wife, because she has conceived what is in her by the Holy Spirit. She will give birth to a son and you must name him Jesus...' When Joseph woke up he did what the angel of the Lord had told him to do: he took his wife to his home and, though he had not had intercourse with her, she gave birth to a son; and he named him Jesus" (Matthew I:20-21 and 24-25).

Joseph decided to adopt Mary's child as his own son. In the eyes of the people, before the law, Jesus would be Joseph's son. The people would refer to Jesus as "the son of Joseph" (John 6:42), and say "this is the carpenter's son" (Matthew 13:55).

Joseph was "presumed" to be the father of Jesus, that is, the supposed father. People assumed and believed that Joseph was the father of Jesus.

In those times, as in ours, genealogies were made from the man's side. Joseph was a descendant of King David, and it was through Joseph, the adoptive father, that Jesus could claim to be a descendant of David.

Joseph decided to adopt Mary's child as his own son. In the eyes of the people, before the law, Jesus would be Joseph's son.

Did Jesus Have Brothers and Sisters?

While remaining a virgin, Mary brought Jesus into the world. There is nothing to prove that she and Joseph had other children.

Church tradition affirms that Mary and Joseph never engaged in sexual relations, but rather lived together as brother and sister. This does not mean that they did not love each other or that they were abnormal! Joseph and Mary were neither "deranged" nor suffering from complexes!

This couple put themselves in the service of the child. Joseph and Mary found their joy in welcoming him and raising him in their tenderness. That is how they found their fulfilment: they were giving everything for Jesus, living only for him.

There are those who say: "Mary did not always remain a virgin." Some have claimed that she had children other than Jesus. But Catholics have traditionally answered: "Joseph and Mary did not have sexual relations. Mary became the mother of Jesus through the action of the Spirit of God and remained a virgin all her life." St. Joseph is often portrayed with a lily in his hand to symbolize his celibate life with Mary.

THE WORD "BROTHER" IN THE BIBLE

In biblical times, as in the Orient today, the word brother can mean son of the same mother, or next of kin.

Thus, Abraham also said to his nephew Lot: "We are brothers" (Genesis 13:8). A little later we again read that Abraham recaptured his "kinsman" Lot (Genesis 14:16). We can see that the word brother and kinsman are used interchangeably.

Referring to a half-brother, a cousin or a nephew as a "brother" was a way of emphasizing the direct lineage between members of the same clan.

Yet, the Gospels of Mark and Matthew speak of the brothers and sisters of Jesus. Consider the following passage about the reaction of the people of Nazareth to the teaching of Jesus: "...and most of them were astonished when they heard him. They said: 'Where did the man get all this? What is this wisdom that has been granted him, and these miracles that are worked through him? This is the carpenter's son, surely, the son of Mary, the brother of James and Joset and Jude and Simon? His sisters, too, are they not here with us?'" (Mark 6:2-3).

If these people were not the brothers and sisters of Jesus, then who were they?

Some speculate that Mary was married to a widower with children. In this case, those whom the Gospels call the "brothers" of Jesus would be sons from Joseph's first marriage. This is not impossible, but the Gospels do not speak of it.

An apocryphal writing, *The History of Joseph the Carpenter*, explains that Joseph married for the first time at the age of forty. After forty-nine years of marriage he became a widower. He remained alone for one year when the priests of the temple entrusted Mary to him. After the third year of her marriage with Joseph, Mary became pregnant with Jesus through the Holy Spirit. According to this imaginative author, Joseph would have been ninety-two years old when Jesus came into the world.

This writing has influenced many artists. It is here that the legend of Joseph as an old man has its beginning. In these pictures, one can easily mistake Joseph for the grandfather of the child he is holding in his arms.

Don't you find something a little strange about this story. When Joseph married Mary, he was surely not an old man who had passed the age for having children. Why? Because this would have been directly contrary to God's plan that Jesus be known as the son of Joseph.

It is not impossible that Joseph had some children from a first marriage and that his second marriage was with Mary. But once again, the Gospels do not tell us this. Those claiming that Mary was the wife of an old man passed the age of having children are not in agreement with the Gospels. No one would believe that Jesus was the son of Joseph. Indeed they could have thought his mother an adulteress!

Still trying to explain why the Gospels speak of the brothers and sisters of Jesus, some people speculate that Joseph had adopted his brother's children. In this way first cousins of Jesus would have become his brothers and sisters through adoption. While this is not impossible, it can't be proven.

We know now that when the Gospels speak of the "brothers" of Jesus, they do not necessarily intend to say that Mary had children other than Jesus. This may be a way of referring to first cousins, being the next of kin.

Though the Gospels speak of the "brothers" of Jesus, this doesn't necessarily mean that Mary had children other than Jesus. The Gospels may be referring to first cousins, being next of kin.

Mary and Joseph: Jesus' First Teachers

Jesus grew up in a family. Mary and Joseph taught him how to walk, speak, pray, work. They did their best to raise Jesus according to their religion and the customs of their nation.

God learned to live like us, even to the point of being a baby who needed us in order to "grow up." We know that a newborn child is weak and has many needs. That is how Jesus was in Bethlehem: a small baby in the arms of Mary and Joseph. He was a small baby who needed milk from his mother and also needed care and tenderness.

Jesus learned the language of his country, with the particular accent of the people of Galilee, from Mary and Joseph. Like the other children of Israel, Jesus learned his first prayers from his mother. Later, he went with his father to the house of prayer — the synagogue — for Bible lessons and religious services.

It is truly astounding when we think about it: the Son of God wanted to take on the limitations of our humanity, of his country, and of the culture that surrounded him.

Mary and Joseph were not highly educated people. They did their best to teach Jesus what they knew. Joseph taught Jesus his trade, and both parents passed on their faith and their attachment to the law of the Lord.

MARY, AN ADMIRABLE EDUCATOR

How astonishing that a woman was able to bring God into the world! Her mission was to raise him as any mother would raise her son, to prepare him for his future activity.

Mary was a perfect mother which is why she was also an admirable educator. The fact, confirmed by the Gospels, that Jesus ''lived under their authority'' (Luke 2:51), shows that her maternal presence had a profound influence on the human development of the Son of God. This is one of the most impressive aspects of the mystery of the Incarnation.

John Paul II, weekly message,
January 4, 1984.

Mary and Joseph found their fulfilment in giving themselves completely to Jesus and living only for him.

The Lesson of Nazareth

By his "ordinary" life at Nazareth, the Saviour showed us the importance of our every-day lives and work. He showed us the grandeur of a simple life when it is lived properly.

Nazareth is a "school," Pope Paul VI told us, and it has some very important things to teach us. We live in a society that judges people by the money they have in the bank, their job, their car and the size of their house. But the reality of Nazareth says this is wrong. Rather, it is the person who is all-important, not things. Our importance lies not in what we have, but in what we are. This is the lesson of Nazareth. Jesus took thirty years of his life to teach this to us.

The life of the Holy Family also teaches us that if we bring goodness and honesty to everything we do — work, rest, prayer, conversation, celebration — then our lives will shine forth with greatness and beauty. This is precious in the eyes of God. Why? Because it involves God's children. We are children of God in everything that happens to us: in our joy and in our pain, in our wedding celebrations and in our mourning.

Let us remember that Mary was just as close to God and just as holy when carrying out her work as a wife and mother of the family as she was by praying in the house or in the synagogue.

The same is true of Jesus. He was as much a son of God while working as a carpenter as when he was preaching along the roads of Galilee. When he ate the meal that his mother had prepared for him, he was as much a son of God as at the multiplication of the loaves.

Our ancestors had a great devotion to "Jesus, Mary and Joseph." Most homes had a picture of the Holy Family. When they gathered to pray, they turned themselves towards Jesus, Mary and Joseph to learn to live their lives serenely and courageously.

Times have changed and so has the way of living. God is not asking us to live as in the times of our ancestors and certainly not as in the time of the Holy Family. But Nazareth can inspire each generation to live in faith, hope and love. It can inspire each one of us, no matter who we are or what we do.

While her life on this earth was like ours, filled with family concerns and tasks, Mary was always intimately united with her Son and co-operated in the work of the Saviour in an altogether special manner.

Vatican Council,
Decree on the Apostolate of the Laity, No. 4.

Chapter 6

The First Believer

Even though life has changed greatly since the time of Mary, certain things have remained the same. She lived her life as we do today, with the same feelings and experiences of faith and devotion. Like us, she did not always understand the teachings of Jesus. Like us, she did not know what the future would hold. Like us, perhaps, she was not always encouraged by her relatives and friends to follow Jesus. The Gospel says that "not even his brothers, in fact, had faith in him" (John 7:5).

Mary was upset at times, as we sometimes are, by incidents in her life. She lived in hope of ascending one day with Christ — like us, like the apostles — without understanding what was meant by the expression "rising from the dead" (Mark 9:10).

Mary Believed First

To believe is to devote ourselves to God, to trust in God's words and promises, to have complete faith in God, to be sure that God cannot deceive us. This is exactly what Mary did.

What does it mean to believe? You could answer that question in any number of ways. To believe is to have faith. To have faith is to believe in what God said to us. It is to know in our hearts and our minds that God is honest with us. It is to believe without having seen for ourselves. It is to have confidence in God. To believe is to trust even when we do not understand. It is to live our lives by observing God's word. To have faith is a gift of God.

Did Mary have faith? When we read the Gospel we realize that Mary lived her life according to God's will. "She lived by faith like us," said Saint Theresa of the Child Jesus, but, like Abraham, without understanding everything, without knowing in advance where this faith would lead.

We are believers, too, just like Mary. But Mary's trust in God and her faithfulness to the Lord were much greater than ours.

She was the first to believe in Jesus. We can see this at the wedding at Cana. It was Mary who told her son that they were out of wine. She said to the servants: "Do whatever he tells you." We know what happened: Jesus changed the water into wine (John 2:1-11).

This was Jesus' first miracle. Because of it, the disciples began to believe in him, but Mary had believed in him long before he performed this first miracle. ''She believed before the others and better than the others'' (John Paul II).

Mary believed before anyone else did and better than anyone else did. She believed before the apostles did.

Even though her relatives did not believe in Jesus, and even though some of his followers had more enthusiasm than faith, Mary's faith remained unshaken.

John Paul II, Notre-Dame du Cap,
September 10, 1984

Nothing Is Impossible to God

Mary believed that what the Lord had promised would be fulfilled in her. She was convinced that "nothing is impossible to God" (Luke 1:37).

When Mary went to visit her cousin, Elizabeth congratulated her for her faith. She said to her: "Yes, blessed are you who believed that the promise made by the Lord would be fulfilled" (Luke 1:45). Yes, Mary deserved to be congratulated for her faith. It was not easy to believe what had been announced to her: that she was to become a mother while remaining a virgin.

She was convinced that "nothing is impossible to God." She knew this from what she had read about the life of Abraham (see Genesis 18:14). But what had been announced to her was so astonishing, so unbelievable!

Mary remembered Abraham to whom God had promised numerous descendants: "Even the thought that his body was past fatherhood — he was about a hundred years old — and Sarah too old to become a mother, did not shake his belief. Since God had promised it, Abraham refused either to deny it or even to doubt it, but drew strength from faith, and gave glory to God, convinced that God had power to do what he had promised" (Romans 4:19-21).

In her profound faith, Mary — like Abraham — knew that God had created the world and everything that exists. Whatever God wills is done. Whatever God promises is fulfilled. God need only say something and it is accomplished. "No sooner said than done." The Holy Spirit, of whom the angel Gabriel speaks, is the power of God who created the universe, starting from nothing.

Mary considered herself unworthy of being the mother of the Messiah. But she trusted in God's promise to be with her. Filled with the Holy Spirit, Mary confidently committed herself, saying "Let what you have said be done to me" (Luke 1:38).

The resemblances between Abraham and Mary are remarkable, especially between the narration of the birth of Isaac, the promised child, and that of the virginal conception of Jesus, the holy son of Mary, woman of faith of the New Testament.

Abraham, our father in the faith, can teach us much about Mary, our mother in the faith.

The U.S. Bishops,
***Behold Your Mother*, No. 30.**

God Speaks through Events

Even during disconcerting events, Mary knew very well that God was present. Despite appearances to the contrary, God was there, very near to her. She was sure of that.

You may have heard the expression, "That was providential." Perhaps you have even said this yourself. After a difficult or disconcerting event, we sometimes find that, in spite of appearances, God was with us and helped us to cope with our problem. Perhaps, at the time, we could not understand what the Lord wanted. Later, we see that the Lord did not forsake us, but was with us. Obviously, we see this through the eyes of faith. Belief is necessary to recognize the Saviour's presence when life is not what we want or expect it to be.

Unbelievers cannot see beyond the present. This is understandable: they are unable to recognize that God is with them since they do not believe in God.

Disconcerting and unsettling experiences can happen to us at any time. Remember what happened to Mary, near the end of her pregnancy, as her delivery time approached. The young couple were preparing themselves for the birth of the baby. That Mary would give birth far away from home, at the other end of the country, was probably the farthest thing from their mind.

Suddenly one day, the Roman Emperor decreed that the people had to go to Bethlehem, the city from which Joseph had come, to take part in a census. Getting there would take four days by caravan. Mary had reached the end of her preganancy...

It must have taken a very strong faith to see the hand of God at work in this decision by the Roman Emperor, a pagan who had conquered Palestine. Yet Mary remained calm: she knew that the Lord, fully aware that the birth of the child was approaching, had not forsaken her.

The public inn in Bethlehem was full, so Mary and Joseph had to find a small corner in a stable and put the little one to sleep in the animal manger. All of this is very beautiful and touching in our Christmas cribs! But imagine how much faith it must have required of Mary to see God's plan unfolding in all of this! To recognize that the baby in the animal manger was the Messiah awaited as the king of Israel: "The Lord God will give him the throne of his ancestor David" (Luke 1:32).

Yes, Mary, you are blessed because you believed that God's promise for you would be fulfilled. God is there, in this baby coming from you. Poor and small, God is in your arms, drinking milk from your breasts.

In our daily lives, we should take time (with Mary) to contemplate the God who is far greater than we, and who, nevertheless, constantly remains near us and loves us.

John Paul II, in Switzerland,
June 5, l984.

They Did Not Understand What Jesus Said to Them

To believe is never easy. This should not surprise us: God is greater than we are. God's ability to understand and to reason surpasses ours. Mary also had to learn to have faith, and it was not easy for her either. But with each passing day she came to understand more clearly the plan of God and the mission of her Son.

To believe is to trust in God even when we do not understand. To have faith is to respond to God who reveals to us his thoughts, plans, and ways of seeing things. If, sometimes, we do not understand God, we should not be surprised. God is much greater than we are — infinitely so.

The Bible tells us: "My thoughts are not your thoughts, my ways not your ways..." (Isaiah 55:8). At times we may be tempted to think that it was different for Mary, that it was easier for her to believe since she lived with Jesus. But to think this way is to forget what faith is, to forget what the Gospels tell us about Mary.

Mary was like us and did not always understand. Even if she was the mother of Jesus and even if she had never sinned, she was still a human being with all the human limitations. Luke's Gospel shows us very clearly that Mary did not always understand the actions and words of Jesus.

LIFE WAS NOT EASY FOR MARY

The perfection accorded to Mary should not give us the impression that her life on this earth was a kind of heavenly life, very different from our own.

In reality, Mary had an existence that was the same as ours. She knew the daily difficulties and trials of human life. She lived with the uncertainties that accompany faith. Like Jesus, she experienced temptation and inner struggles. We can imagine how she was overcome by the dramatic passion of her Son. It would be an error to think that the life of the one who was full of grace was easy or comfortable.

Mary shared everything that belongs to our earthly condition, with its needs and suffering.

John Paul II, weekly message,
December 7, 1983.

Let us recall the family's pilgrimage to Jerusalem, when Jesus was twelve years old. Instead of returning with his parents, he stayed in the holy city. It took three days of looking before Mary and Joseph found him again, in the temple. Mary said: "My child, why have you done this to us?" Jesus answered: "Did you not know that I had to be in my Father's house?" To this Luke added: "But they did not understand what he meant" (Luke 2:48-50).

What they did not understand was what Jesus meant by saying: "I must be in my Father's house." The twelve-year-old child said that God was his Father and that he must be with his Father. This meant that he had to dedicate himself to the work of his Father. He had to serve his Father to the end, until the cross.

By his resurrection, he would find himself again "with the Father." We can see that this response of Jesus could be understood only after his death and resurrection.

His mother did not know how Jesus would accomplish his mission. She could not foresee that he would be rejected by his own people and put to death, nor could she know in advance that he would rise to be in glory "with the Father."

We can understand Mary and Joseph's reaction to Jesus' response. They reacted like the disciples did when Jesus announced to them, for the third time, his passion, death and resurrection: "But they could make nothing of this; what he said was quite obscure to them, they had no idea what it meant" (Luke 18:34).

Once again, these words could not be understood except after the resurrection and ascension of Jesus. That's why Mary and Joseph were unable to understand the meaning of the words when Jesus actually spoke to them.

Mary's reaction to the words and actions of her Son are very instructive. The Gospel tells us: "Mary treasured all these things... and pondered them in her heart" (Luke 2:19). She meditated on the things that she did not understand the first time. She reflected on what had happened and on what Jesus had said.

This is how, over the days and the years, she came to better understand Jesus and his mission. It was by meditating on the word of God, in order to live it better, that she grew in her faith.

And what about us? We, who are sometimes confused by God's plans, and who do not always understand what God is doing and what God wants to tell us. Let us not forget Mary's "secret." Let us follow her example and wait for the Holy Spirit to enlighten the eyes of our heart.

(Mary is) blessed because she "has believed," and she continues to believe, day after day, amidst all the trials and adversities of Jesus' infancy and then during the years of the hidden life at Nazareth where he was "obedient to them" (Luke 2:51).

John Paul II,
Redemptoris Mater, No. 17.

The Secret of Mary's Greatness

What is it that makes Mary so great: the fact of being Jesus' mother, or of being his disciple? Saint Augustine answered: what makes Mary great is first of all her faith in Christ.

Mary played a unique role in the history of the world: she gave birth to the Son of God. She raised him to adulthood. This is an incomparable honour. Later, she followed her Son and became his first disciple. We could ask what it was that brought Jesus and Mary so close: her parentage by blood or her faith in him?

Saint Augustine said that Mary was more blessed for believing in Christ than for conceiving him. And he added: "The maternal bond would have been of little special value to Mary had she not felt happier to receive Christ in her heart than in her body."

Jesus himself said the same thing. "Now as he was speaking, a woman in the crowd raised her voice and said, 'Happy the womb that bore you and the breasts you sucked!' But he replied, 'Still happier those who hear the word of God and keep it'" (Luke 11:27-28).

Jesus, of course, was not negating Mary's happiness at having brought Jesus into the world. But, in his eyes, there was a greater relationship between him and his mother than the relationship of blood. Mary is close to her Son and her God because she puts his word into practice. This is the only way in which we can be close to Jesus and be one with him: by doing what God asks.

BLESSED BECAUSE OF HER FAITH

Without any doubt, Mary is worthy of blessing by the very fact that she became the mother of Jesus according to the flesh (''Blessed is the womb that bore you and the breasts that you sucked''), and especially because already at the Annunciation she accepted the word of God, because she believed it, because she was obedient to God, and because she ''kept'' the word and ''pondered it in her heart,'' and by means of her whole life accomplished it.

Jean Paul II,
Redemptoris Mater, No. 20.

Jesus was very clear on this: ''Anyone who does the will of God...is my brother and sister and mother'' (Mark 3:35). This is also true for Mary. This is why Jesus said in front of the whole crowd that Mary was blessed: because she is one of those who ''hear the word of God and keep it'' (Luke 11:28).

She took to heart what Jesus said. When Jesus was small, Mary nourished and educated him. Now that he had grown and had announced the Good News of the Kingdom, she accepted being nourished and instructed by her Son. She paid attention to every word he uttered. Nothing would be lost. Every word would light her way.

All her life, she repeated in her heart the Good News that Jesus had proclaimed on the mountain:

"How happy are the poor in spirit;
theirs is the kingdom of heaven.
Happy the gentle:
they shall have the earth for their heritage.
Happy those who mourn:
they shall be comforted.
Happy those who hunger and thirst for what is right:
they shall be satisfied.
Happy the merciful:
they shall have mercy shown to them.
Happy the pure of heart:
they shall see God.
Happy the peacemakers:
they shall be called children of God.
Happy those who are persecuted in the cause of right:
theirs is the kingdom of heaven.

"Happy are you when people abuse you and persecute you and speak all kinds of calumny against you on my account. Rejoice and be glad, for your reward will be great in heaven..." (Matthew 5:3-12).

Patiently (Mary) followed her "pilgrimage of faith" up to the foot of her Son's cross. On this route, she unites with us: a mother, a sister, who thinks and lives with us.

John Paul II, in Switzerland,
June 5, 1984.

The mother of Jesus was happy to see and hear these things. Many prophets and holy people longed to see what she saw, and did not see, to hear what she heard, and did not hear (see Matthew 13:16-17). With Mary, the seed of the Kingdom fell on good earth. Her good and generous heart received it and bore fruit by its perseverance (see Luke 8:5). She is the first to put into practice the words spoken to the servants at the wedding: "Do whatever he tells you" (John 2:5).

A Symbol of Strength and Hope

In times of difficulty, it is not easy to believe that God is with us. It is difficult for us to continue thinking that God is near, when sometimes God seems to be far away. We are tempted to ask ourselves if God really knows what is happening.

"How could this happen? If God loves us, how can anyone explain what happened to me? I who try so hard to practice my religion and to do what God asks of me..." It is difficult to understand why our faith can be tested so severely. Why does it always seem that everything goes well for those who do not believe?

This is something like what happened at Calvary. On Good Friday afternoon, everything seemed to be a failure. The crowds that had followed and applauded Jesus were no longer there. Even the apostles were hiding, except John. Only a handful of people were with Jesus on that afternoon: Mary, some other women and John, the disciple.

High on the cross was Jesus, seemingly powerless. Below, his adversaries were snickering and rubbing their hands. They jeered and said: "Aha! So you would destroy the Temple and rebuild it in three days! Then save yourself! If you are God's son, come down from the cross.... He saved others; he cannot save himself.... Let him come down from the cross now, and we will believe in him. He puts his trust in God; now let God rescue him if he wants him" (Matthew 27:39-43).

People were saying: "If God is doing nothing for him, that proves that everything he said was false. He was a liar. He was not a prophet of God. God is not with him. He is not a friend of God since God did not come to rescue him!" Jesus was abandoned. The "powerful ones" had the upper hand.

A "sword" pierced the heart of Mary. She saw the Just One delivered to the persecution of his enemies, good destroyed by the wicked. People said that God had forgotten his Son, that God no longer cared for him.

What a terrible test this was for Mary's faith! She had always believed that God was on the side of the just and the weak and that God did not forsake those who placed their trust in him. When Jesus was small, she helped him to understand the psalms. With him, she sang: "God will free the poor and those who need help; he will have pity on the poor and feeble, and save the lives of those in need..." (Psalm 72:12-13).

But here was her Son, overcome by the power of evildoers, yet God remained silent and did nothing! She was so joyful in her *Magnificat* because God chased away those with arrogant hearts. She had sung: "He has pulled down princes from their thrones and exalted the lowly." Was the *Magnificat* a "lie" because of what happened at Calvary, because Jesus fell into the hands of the arrogant and powerful and God did not intervene?

Mary had the good fortune
to carry in her womb
under her heart
and later in her arms
the Son of God our Saviour.

She received him for the last time
in her arms at Calvary
when they took him down from the cross.

They wrapped him in a sheet
and carried him to the tomb
before the very eyes of his mother.
(John Paul II)

Had she been mistaken? This all seemed so scandalous: the Just One had been abandoned to the hands of sinners. This is so difficult to understand. If it is really true that God is good, why does God allow the poor to suffer? Why does God allow the big to crush the small? Yet many who are humiliated and rejected by their fellow creatures remain faithful to God. It all seems so revolting and shocking to see good people exploited by others with no conscience.

And God seems to let things happen that way! For a while it is the hour of darkness. A woman mourns for her Son. Jesus is dead, but in her heart, the mother continues to hope. Then there is no more hope: they have just closed Jesus' tomb. "My life... I lay it down of my own free will, and as it is in my power to lay it down, so it is in my power to take it up again" (John 10:17-18). It is night and these words of Jesus come back to comfort her heart and mind. It is night and Mary remains loyal.

What a lesson of strength and hope she gave us by standing near the cross at the moment when the mission of her Son appeared to be collapsing and ending in dishonour.

The Quebec Bishops,
The Virgin Mary in Christian Life
in Quebec Today*, No. 16.*

The Joy of Easter

God did not abandon Jesus. The Father heard the prayer of his Son. He raised him from the dead and brought him into a new life. What a joy for his mother: Jesus would never again suffer or die! He is living forever!

When we love someone, we suffer when we see that person suffer. But also, the more we love someone, the more we rejoice at his good fortune. We can imagine Mary's joy on Easter morning: the one she loves so much is now protected from all suffering. Never again will death be able to touch him.

The joy of Easter — Jesus has gained the upper hand over our three greatest enemies: Satan, sin, and death. There is joy because the seed, thrown on the earth at Calvary, has now borne fruit: new life! What Jesus said to his disciples has been realized: "Your sorrow will turn to joy.... I shall see you again, and your hearts will be full of joy, and that joy no one shall take from you" (John 16:20, 22).

Did Jesus appear to his mother as he did to his disciples? The Gospels do not tell us. Some people think that he manifested himself in a special way to his mother. This is possible, but Mary does not seem to have spoken about it. One thing is certain: Mary "knew" that Jesus was living. In faith, she "experienced" his new presence, which was different from what it was before. As with the disciples and us, only through faith could Mary know that Jesus had risen from the dead.

ALLELUIA!

As a daughter of Israel, Mary knew the psalms by heart. Psalms are prayers inspired by the Holy Spirit. This psalm, used for the great liturgical feasts in Jerusalem, was sung by the first believers in the risen Jesus, and Mary was there.

I will thank you for you have answered me
and you are my saviour.

The stone which the builders rejected
has become the cornerstone.
This is the work of the Lord,
a marvel in our eyes.
This day was made by the Lord;
we rejoice and are glad!

Give thanks to the Lord for he is good;
for his love endures for ever.

(Psalm 118:21-24, 29).

We cannot recognize the risen Christ except in faith. Unbelievers saw nothing. This was as true then as it is today. But those who believe do not look for Jesus among the dead. They know he is living and that he accompanies them. "Happy are those who have not seen and yet believe" (John 20:29).

Mary Meets Jesus in the Church

As with us today, Mary could meet the risen Christ in the community of disciples, in prayer, in the word of God, and in the sacraments.

We might think that Mary had the opportunity to see and talk with Jesus. It is true that Mary had lived closer to the Son of God than any other person. Nevertheless, before he left, Jesus said: "It is for your good that I am going....When the Spirit of truth comes he will lead you to the complete truth" (John 16:7, 13). If it was "advantageous" for his disciples — and his mother — that Jesus left, it was because he intended something for them that would be even greater than his earthly presence.

Even this Mary received with faith. Though unable to understand perfectly, she was certain that it was a good thing for her and the disciples that Jesus was going away. But how could this come about?

From the day of the Annunciation, it was by the Holy Spirit that the Son of God had begun his human life in Mary. From the day of Pentecost, by the same Holy Spirit, Jesus came to live even more intimately in the heart of his mother. The risen Saviour would be still closer than when he was living on earth. He would now no longer be *with* us, but *in* us. By the Holy Spirit, Jesus would live in the very depths of our heart.

The assembled community received the outpouring of the Holy Spirit. The apostles were transformed: boldly they proclaimed that Jesus lives and that he is truly the one whom God sent as the Saviour of the world.

Mary was not one of the apostles. Jesus did not commission her to preach. What then is her place according to the Gospel? It is to live, from day to day, "in her place simply as one of the faithful, but the first among the faithful as their mother" (John Paul II), in the midst of the community.

When speaking of the faith of Mary after Easter, we should not forget that she could meet Jesus in exactly the same way that we can today: in others, in prayer, in the word of God, and in the sacraments. For his mother, this meeting with Jesus in the Church was even more profound, more intimate, than when she carried him within her, or when she lived beside him at Nazareth.

This came to be by the coming of the Holy Spirit. This is also what Jesus had in mind when he said to his disciples: "It is better for you that I go away." This helps us to understand one thing: Jesus wants to be in his Church, and we can meet him there.

At her place as any one of the faithful, but as the first among the faithful because she was the mother of Jesus, (Mary) joined in common prayer. She united her voice to those of the apostles and the other disciples in asking for the gift of the Holy Spirit. The same Spirit had overshadowed her at the Annunciation, making her the mother of God.

John Paul II, Regina Coeli,
May 22, 1983.

I would be wrong if I pretended that I could "by-pass" the Church, if I thought that we did not need the disciples of Jesus — that is, the Church — to meet him and to enter into the salvation that he has brought us. Jesus is "married" to the Church. This means married to his disciples in each generation. It is there, in the Church, in the community, that he acts and comes to us. This is where we can meet him. This was true for Mary, and it is true for us today.

A Resurrection Faith

Jesus' promise was extraordinary: "I am going to prepare a place for you, and after I have gone and prepared you a place, I shall return to take you with me; so that where I am you may be too" (John 14:2-3). Without knowing how this could come about, Mary believed that God could raise the dead to life. It is the same for us: we believe, not because we understand, but because we know that God can do whatever he says.

When we recall the words of Elizabeth — "Blessed is she who believed" (Luke 1:45) — we think first of all of Mary's faith on the day of the Annunciation. We could perhaps say to ourselves: "We are not in the same situation as Mary. God entrusted her with a special role. It is not the same for us..." This is true, but don't forget the promise that Jesus made to his mother and to all of us.

What is this promise? It is to raise us up after our death. Do you think Mary understood how this was going to happen? As with us and the apostles, she did not understand — no more than on the day of the Annunciation. None of us can understand how we will rise. In all of this, we are like Mary and she is like us. However, with this incredible promise of resurrection, Mary had the same conviction as at the Annunciation: "...nothing is impossible to God" (Luke 1:37).

The example of Mary's faith can help us to believe and to maintain hope in spite of everything. We are all alike: none of us can understand how the dead will leave the cemetery. Mary did not believe because she understood what God had said, but because she was sure of God. She knew that God could not deceive us and would not forsake us, and that whatever God had promised, God would do.

As Mary neared the end of her life, she continued to do what she had always done: she recalled and pondered in her heart the words and the actions of Jesus. She did not forget what he said: "I am going now to prepare a place for you, and after I have gone and prepared you a place, I shall return to take you with me; so that where I am you may be too" (John 14:2-3). With all her being she says to him: "Amen; come, Lord Jesus!" (Revelation 22:20).

Nothing is impossible to God, except deceit. Let us renew our faith in God and remember that everything is within God's reach."

Saint Clement of Rome

Chapter 7

Body and Soul in Heaven

Our faith tells us that Mary is very much alive. She is living like Jesus is since Easter. The Son has taken his mother "body and soul" into the life of God. This is what we call the "Assumption" of Mary.

This same life has also been promised to us when, in the end, Christ will come to make "the new heavens and the new earth" (2 Peter 3:13).

Like the Risen Christ

To understand what happened to Mary in her Assumption, we must look at the risen Jesus. Like him, she will live forever, free from suffering and death.

We know that Jesus left the tomb in order to enter into a new life. He rose as a man filled with the life of God. With Easter, the human capacities of Jesus were expanded. He could transcend space, and he was no longer limited by time. Jesus today can be everywhere at the same time. His humanity has been flooded with the power of the Spirit of God, and that is why he can no longer suffer or die.

Why is it important to look at the risen Christ? Because he realized his full potential — something God wants all of us to do. The risen Jesus is our future. We will become like him if we let God realize in us what he has promised.

God's plan is to raise all those who are among the dead. Jesus was the first. We, too, are to rise like Jesus, each in our turn.

Do you realize how astounding that is? When people die, they are taken to the cemetery. We can do nothing for them anymore. They are dead. This is why the announcement of our resurrection is so astonishing.

To nourish our hope, we should always remember what God told us: "If the Spirit of him who raised Jesus from the dead is living in you, then he who raised Jesus from the dead will give life to your own mortal bodies through the Spirit living in you" (Romans 8:11).

This is what happened to Mary by her Assumption. The Holy Spirit, which made her body fruitful with Jesus, has made this same body live forever. The Spirit of the living God, who created Mary in the first place, has re-created her according to the model of the risen Christ.

The risen Jesus is our future. We will become like him if we let God realize in us what he has promised.

God Made Us Body and Soul

Materialists say: "We are nothing more than a body." Those who believe in reincarnation, answer: "No, we are nothing but a spirit. The body is not part of our person. It is only an envelope for our spirit." As Christians we know God has made us body and soul. It is in our whole being, body and soul, that God wishes us to live with him. For Jesus, there is no such thing as reincarnation. Nor is there for us. When we speak of the "other life," we mean being body and soul in the joy of the Lord, as Mary is today.

Materialists deny the existence of the soul and of God. That is why they say: "We are only a body." This is not correct: we are also a spirit. We are matter and spirit, that is, body and soul. We are not just a spirit, as those who believe in reincarnation contend. (Reincarnation means a new entry of the spirit into the flesh, into the body.) For these people, the human being is just a "spirit" that could exist by itself, but which is "enclosed" in a body on the earth. For them, the body is not part of our person. It is nothing but a skin, a peel, a shell, or an envelope.

What happens, then, when someone comes into the world? People who believe in reincarnation will answer: a spirit, a being that existed previously, enters into an envelope that we call the body. This may be the first, second, third or fourth time that this spirit is imprisoned in a body. Each time, the body — the envelope, the shell — changes. The shell can be the body of a man or the body of a woman. In another reincarnation it could be the body of an animal. It all depends...

What happens when someone dies? The same people will answer: "The spirit is freed from its prison, but since it must carry the weight of its bad actions, it is condemned to enter again into another prison. In other words, it must reincarnate until it is perfect." As you can see, being reincarnated isn't much fun. It is a burden to carry, a consequence of the evil that someone may have done.

This belief is not consistent with the Gospel. Reincarnation is contrary to the teaching of Jesus. We come into the world once. We do not have several lives, but only one. After this, our "other life" will depend on how we welcomed Christ and others in this present life.

For Jesus, we are neither just a spirit nor just a body. We consist of both. For God, the human body is more than an envelope. It is part of our being. The body that was formed in the womb of the Virgin Mary was more than a "skin" for the Son of God. That human body was Christ himself. That is why he went to heaven with his risen body. It is with his body that "he sits at the right hand of the Father." To be at the Father's "right hand" means to be equal to God.

When God offers to free us from everything that could harm or destroy us, it is to save us "completely," so to speak, to free our soul and our body. This is what God did to Mary: with her whole being she entered into the life of God. She was "embraced in her body and in her soul by the mystery of the living God: of the Father, the Son and the Holy Spirit" (John Paul II).

If we are serious, we cannot believe in the Resurrection of Jesus and the Assumption of Mary, and believe at the same time in reincarnation. These beliefs do not go together; they contradict each other.

Mary Awaits Us

At the end of the road, Mary is beckoning us. She encourages us to walk on the road that she herself has followed. As we behold Mary living close to God, our life and our future become clear: we can see where the road that Jesus has shown us will lead.

One day, together with our mother, we shall be like God, because we shall see God as God really is (see 1 John 3:2).

Some thought that Mary did not die, but that she was taken into heaven without dying. Pope Pius XII avoided the issue when he proclaimed the dogma of the Assumption. If Mary did not die, she would, nevertheless, have had to be transformed in her whole being in order to become like the risen Jesus. This transformation would have been so profound that it would have been a resurrection.

Our mortal body must become immortal. It must be renewed to the point where it can no longer suffer and die. Eternal life is a completely new way of existing. It is into this new way of being that Jesus brought Mary immediately at the end of her life. In other words: Jesus exempted his mother from the grave and allowed her to pass immediately to heavenly life.

THE ASSUMPTION OF MARY IS PART OF THE CATHOLIC FAITH

Pope Pius XII solemnly defined the Assumption on November 1, 1950: "We affirm, we declare, and we define as a divinely revealed dogma that: the immaculate mother of God, Mary ever virgin, after having completed the course of her earthly life, was taken body and soul into heavenly glory."

The good news for us is that what happened to Mary will happen to us when Christ comes to make "the new heavens and new earth" (2 Peter 3:13). Therefore, it is to the same Kingdom, where Mary already finds herself, that we will one day also be led. There is not a "special" heaven for the mother of Jesus and another for other humans. To be in heaven is to see God and be with God, to share God's life and happiness forever. It means to be with Jesus at the wedding table, "all together and for eternity," as we say in the Mass.

Mary entered before us and awaits us. Having arrived at the end of the road, she encourages us and beckons to us. It is truly encouraging, in fact, to see one of us already close to God. This is proof that God never breaks promises, that God's word is always kept.

The Lord has set before us "life and happiness, death and disaster" (Deuteronomy 30:15). Mary chose life and happiness. As the Gospel says, those who lose their life for Jesus will gain eternal life (Matthew 10:39). This is exactly what Mary did.

Obviously, this is demanding. But we are not alone: God is with us as he was with Mary. Yes, life is difficult, for it is a "narrow gate" (Matthew 7:13). Mary knows that because she lived through it. She does not regret anything. She does not regret having hoped in the Lord, for she was not deceived. God does not deceive anyone. Mary knows that because she sees it with her own eyes: "What we suffer in this life can never be compared to the glory as yet unrevealed which is waiting for us" (Romans 8:18).

What happened to Mary with the Assumption lights our life and our future. In each of us there is a seed of eternal life that is in the process of germinating and growing. One day it will bear fruit. When Mary was taken body and soul, God showed us what our future would be.

Mary is "the first of the saved." By looking at her, we have an idea of what God wishes to accomplish in each one of us. By looking at Mary who has entered into heaven, we see the plan of God fulfilled.

Mary is the kind of human being whom God "dreamed of" the first morning of creation. She is the human being who perfectly resembles the risen Jesus. In her, humanity is already sharing in the joy of God. One from among us is already benefitting fully from what God wishes to give to all humanity.

Let us not forget that we are already children of God. The Spirit carries out God's work in us. The life of God today works within us. On the "Great Day" this life will shine forth. Then, like Mary, we will be like the Lord: living and free, because we will see him as he is (see 1 John 3:2).

Mary is the "first of the saved." By looking at Mary, we already have an idea of what God wants to accomplish in each one of us.

Part Two

SHE IS ALSO OUR MOTHER

**Holy Mary, mother of God,
pray for us sinners,
now and at the hour of our death.**

Chapter 8

Entrusted to Her

If we are children of God today, it is because Jesus, the good Shepherd, laid down his life for his sheep (John 10:11). Completely in accord with the sentiments of her Son, Mary accepted that he sacrifice himself for us.

At Calvary, the dying Jesus entrusted us to her. Since that day, for our happiness and our consolation, Mary is our mother. She is the mother of the Church, of all the brothers and sisters of her firstborn Son.

"This Is Your Son"

Mary accepted that Jesus would go to the limit by giving his life for those he loved. It is in this manner, by consenting to the offering of her Son, that she helps us "to be born" to the new life that springs from the cross of the Saviour. The dying Jesus asked her to take care of us — to make the life of the children of God grow in us.

"Woman, this is your son" (John 19:26). Mary will never forget these words! Never will she forget the day when her Son died to give us life. That day Jesus asked her to do for us what she had done for him: to love and protect us, and to help us to grow in life. This happened at Calvary at the moment when Jesus gave his life for the salvation of the world.

Jesus looked at his mother and then at John, the disciple: "This is your son... This is your mother." The Son wanted to have his mother there, near him. He wanted her to unite in his sacrifice and co-operate till the end of his mission. His mission was to give us the life of God. This was the reason for his coming: "...so that we may have life" (John 10:10).

At Calvary, Jesus is at the height of his mission: it is his "hour." The hour of his death is when he can accomplish what he came to do: to give us life. It is of this hour that he spoke to his mother at Cana: "Woman, my hour has not come yet" (John 2:4). This hour arrived on Good Friday. Mary was there, united with Jesus in suffering, but also in faith.

MOTHER OF THE NEW LIFE IN US

The person who gave us life was not Mary, but our earthly mother. In addition to the earthly life which our mother gave us, there is another life: the one which comes from Jesus. Thanks to him, we are born a second time: we have become children of God. This is where Mary becomes our mother: she collaborated with Jesus to give us a new life, to make it grow within us.

She agreed to lose her Son and consented that he give his life for us so we could be born to a new life. Furthermore, by saying "yes" to the sacrifice of her Son, Mary took part in our new birth.

What is this new life that God has given us through Jesus? It is a new capacity to know and love God and each other. Mary was the first to receive this life of grace. From the beginning of her existence, God filled her with a "divine ability" for knowing and loving. Because she was the "first of the redeemed," the first to benefit from the salvation made possible through her Son, she is responsible for watching over us, and for helping us grow in our life as children of God. She is our mother!

Because she is the "first of the redeemed," the first to benefit from salvation through her Son, Mary sees herself as having the responsibility to watch over us and to help us grow in life as children of God.

Mary is not our earthly mother as she was for Jesus, but our spiritual mother. She is the mother of the divine grace in us, of the new life that comes to us from the Spirit that Jesus gives to those who belong to him.

Mother of the Church

Jesus wanted to be one with his disciples and he "grafted" us to him. Together with him, we form one "body." Mary is the mother of the whole body: she is mother of Christ and mother of the members of his body. This is why we call her "the mother of the Church."

Jesus gave his life for us to gather us into one "family." He asked his mother to become the mother of all these people! I can say that Mary is my mother, and that is true. I am a child of Mary. "Here is your son," Jesus said from the cross, and Mary adopted each one of us individually.

It is important to remember that on Calvary John represented all the disciples of the future. Jesus asked his mother to adopt all the children of God that he would bring together by his death and resurrection. The children of God gathered by Jesus are the Church: "the community of those who believe and hope, of those who live by the energy that comes from the cross of Christ" (John Paul II).

With her Son, Mary suffered for the Church. With him, she committed herself to watching over the new People of God. The Shepherd is Jesus, but the mother is Mary.

And the "others" who are not believers, what about them? Is Mary also their mother? Mary is the mother of all. All humanity is called to become part of the Body of Christ, to become part of the Church. We also know that Mary loves all those Jesus loves. Her maternal heart does not set anyone aside. By agreeing to give birth to the Saviour, she agreed to become the mother of all those who "were to become one" with Jesus.

I consecrate the whole world, all the nations of the earth, all people to the mother of Christ, because she is everyone's mother.

John Paul II, weekly speech,
May 2, 1979.

Our Sister Too!

It may seem strange to think of Mary as our mother *and* our sister. We have seen how she is our mother, but how can she also be our sister? First of all, Mary is part of the human family and, on this level, she is our sister. In heaven, she is the closest to Jesus, but she also continues to be "on our side." She is always one of us. Because of her special calling, our sister has become our mother. She has become the mother of the Church.

This does not mean that she is above the Church! It would be a very strange way to honour our mother if we put her outside the family! The Church is the "family" of the disciples of Jesus. Mary, the first of the disciples, is part of the family. The life of a child of God, which she received in advance, is a fruit of the cross of her Son. The Virgin Mary is thus a member of the Mystical Body of Christ. She is a member of the Church of which she is the mother.

Because Mary is a disciple of Jesus, she can be called a "daughter of the Church," and equally our "sister." Like us she has been redeemed by Christ, although in an eminent and privileged way.

The U.S. Bishops,
***Behold Your Mother**, No. 114.*

Chapter 9

She Does Not Forget Us

God made Mary with a mother's heart. From God she received the love and tenderness with which she surrounds us. In heaven she thinks of us and intercedes for us. It is not as though there were a void between us and Christ. There is no void: we have direct access to Christ.

Jesus invites his disciples to collaborate with him and to help each other by praying for one another. This support continues in heaven where our brothers and sisters pray for us before God. In this "communion of saints," Mary is the first and the most active.

Like God: Merciful and Good

We call Mary the "mother of mercy" because God made her gracious and good. Mary received her goodness from the Father of mercy from whom comes every perfect gift.

"Would you rather be judged by Mary than by God?" A priest I know asked this question in a parish assembly.

"Oh, yes, certainly," someone answered. "I feel that she would understand me. I would be more at ease with her. The Blessed Virgin is good. She is the mother of mercy."

"What about God?" the priest asked. "Do you think that God does not understand you? Do you think that God is not as 'good' as Mary or less merciful than her?"

What is your answer to these questions? If yes, why? If no, why?

Some people compare our relations with God and Mary to what sometimes happens in a family. They might say, for example: "In our family, the children are often more at ease with mother than with father. When they want something, instead of asking father directly, they will go through mother. She has a way of speaking to father. She has the best chance of getting him to say yes."

Can we use this analogy when speaking of God and of the Virgin Mary? No, not really. We can't use as our point of departure the psychology of children in relation to their parents. We would be acting as if our relations with God and the Virgin Mary were the same. Look closely at what would happen if that were the case.

It is often said that children are less at ease with their fathers than with their mothers. The mother is more understanding and more tender than the father. A mother has the "know-how." If I say that the same is true of God and Mary, do I mean that Mary is more understanding, more tender than God, and that God holds the stick for punishment?

The danger in such a view is that we see God as a very stern father who frightens his children. We deprive God of, and give to Mary, all the "maternal" qualities of tenderness, understanding and mercy. We must be careful not to confuse our faith with family psychology! Clearly, we can have confidence in Mary since she is our mother, and we can be certain that she understands us. But if our way of thinking leads us to believe that Mary understands us better than God, that she is kinder than God, then we're on the wrong road. We'd no longer be speaking of the God of the Bible and of the God of our faith. A God we have clothed with our faults is no longer the true God, but a figment of our imagination.

For the child in your arms
Who laughs and cries
And no longer wishes to be silent
For the child in your arms
And his alleluia
I greet you Mary.

For the child who comes again
Who each morning
Makes the light sing
For the child who comes again
Who will take us with him tomorrow
I greet you Mary.

(André Dumont, OMI)

This does not mean that Mary lacks the ''heart of a mother'' or that she is not full of tenderness and mercy. The Virgin Mary is very kind to her children. There is no doubt about it. However, we should not forget that Mary received her kindness and her good qualities from the God of tenderness and love.

God is love and God made Mary with a heart ''as big as the world'' in the divine image and likeness.

God is love, and God made Mary in the divine image and likeness.

Everything Happens through Jesus

Between God and us is a great and infinite distance. Jesus is the bridge. Through him a passage is established — from God to us and from us to God. Everything happens through Jesus. This is what we mean when we call him the "mediator" between God and us.

When we say that Mary "intercedes" for us, it is important not to think that she comes to fill the "void" between the Lord and us. Mary does not come to replace a rung in the ladder by which we climb to God. True, there is an infinite distance between God and creation. But Jesus removes this distance, not Mary! She is a human creature like us and there is also an infinite distance between her and the Creator. As with us, she needs Jesus to have access to God.

It is Jesus who leads us to his Father from whom life comes. Jesus gives everyone — his mother and us — the life of God which is in his glorified body.

JESUS THE MEDIATOR

Jesus is now interceding for us. This is what the Bible tells us: "...he is living forever to intercede for all who come to God through him" (Hebrews 7:25). It is through Jesus that we can return to God. He is the "bridge" between his Father and us. We need a bridge because we are not on the same shore as God. God is on the other side, or the other bank, so to speak.

Jesus "straddles the stream," with one foot on each bank. He is on our side and God's side at the same time. He can take us by one hand, and his Father by the other hand. He is also a "link" between the Creator and us. Thanks to Jesus, we have direct access to God. With such a mediator, there is no longer a gap between the Father and us.

Some Catholics seem to have forgotten this. They know that Jesus has saved us, but they forget that today he still gives us this salvation brought about by his death and resurrection. Some people also think that he has stopped being a man! One day I asked a group: "Where did Jesus go after the Ascension?" Someone answered: "He became God as he was before!" As far as that person was concerned, in heaven Jesus is no longer a human being. But no, Jesus remains a human being eternally and he will always be the Son of Mary. Christ saves us today by his glorified humanity. All the graces coming to us from the Father pass through him.

The Bible tells us that all graces come to us from the Father through Jesus Christ. Jesus is the *mediator* of all graces. All prayer and all good things that go from the earth to heaven, pass through him as well. This is why we say in the Mass: "Through him, with him, in him... all glory and honour are yours, almighty Father..."

It is as a man that Jesus has taken his seat at the right hand of the Father; it is as a man that he can intercede for us.

The U.S. Bishops,
***Behold Your Mother**, No. 85.*

The Communion of Saints

No one is an island. We are in solidarity with one another. This is also true in our life as children of God. United with Jesus, we rely on one another and we can help one another on our march to the Kingdom. This mutuality, this sharing, is called the "communion of saints," of which Mary is clearly a part.

As children of God we are united to one another. The Lord could well have done everything alone, but instead offered us the opportunity to collaborate in establishing the Kingdom. Jesus was helped by his apostles. He asked them to continue his work. Today, through his disciples, the Lord is made known, and people are helped to answer his call.

For example, how did you learn about Christ? Think of all those who have spoken to you of him and who have helped you in your life of faith. Perhaps they have helped by their example, or perhaps it was by their teaching or their prayers. Just think of all the people without whom you would not have had the good fortune of knowing Jesus! A grandfather or grandmother, a priest or teacher...

Even today, you cannot live your life of faith without others. Why? Because Christ wants to come to you through your brothers and sisters. You also need others to meet the Lord in the sacraments.

As Christians we help each other in many ways. For example, parents raise their children in the faith by showing them how to pray and behave as Jesus taught us: by being of service, being honest, sharing with others, and so on. When children have grown, parents continue to be concerned about their salvation, and they pray for them. We know how grandparents pray for their children and their grandchildren...

The pope and the bishops have the responsibility to call us to be Christians and to guide us on the road of faith. The priests are there to teach us the word of God, to celebrate the sacraments and help us to follow Jesus. All of this creates a divine flow of life between us and God. It is one of the greatest acts of sharing.

This wondrous and beautiful sharing is called the "communion of saints." "Communion" implies a deep union among us. Communion of "saints" means that it is a union of those that Christ has sanctified in the Holy Spirit. This relationship between the members of the Church is a part of our faith. We say in the *Creed*, "I believe in the communion of saints."

Obviously, in wishing to help one another in our life of faith, we do not pretend to confer the salvation of God on our brothers and sisters. God freely comes to us; we do not make God come. God has saved us freely, all of us. Nevertheless, God depends upon human disciples to act as intermediaries, as "roads" to lead God to their brothers and sisters.

This does not end with death. God wants those who have helped others during their life to continue doing so in heaven with all their riches of love and life. The love of God filling their hearts drives them to always help others. They continue to be "charitable" and interested in us.

Near the end of her life Saint Theresa of the Child Jesus prophesied: "I have many things I want to do once I get to heaven...I will begin my mission by making others love God as I love God and by giving my secret 'little way' to souls. If God grants my wishes, my heaven will be spent on earth until the end of the world. Yes, I want to spend my heaven doing good on earth."

We all know what happened. Theresa of Lisieux did not sit around idly with her arms crossed! Since her death, she has taught us how to become children of God so we can enter the Kingdom of Heaven. Saint Theresa is proof that those who are with the Father in heaven remain united with their brothers and sisters on earth.

To what extent can I help others gain their salvation? Only God can answer this question. But we do know one thing: the closer we are to God, in faith and love, the closer we are to one another.

Think about the spokes of a bicycle wheel. The closer the spokes are to the centre, the closer they are to one another. We are the spokes of the wheel, and the centre is Christ. The closer we are to him, the closer we are to one another.

The closer we are to Christ, the more we can be "useful" to others in the communion of saints.

This means that the person in the Church who can help us the most is the Virgin Mary because she is the nearest to God and, at the same time, the nearest to us. In the communion of saints, Mary is the most active and the most "useful" to her brothers and sisters who are at the same time her children.

When we help one another with our prayers and our actions on earth, we can count on the saints in heaven, especially on the Blessed Virgin Mary, to help us with their prayers.

The U.S. Bishops,
Behold Your Mother, No. 84.

“Pray for Us Sinners”

Mary wants what is best for us, which is what God wants. United to her Son, Jesus, and one with him in her love for us, Mary obtains for us whatever we need to live as children of God.

How does Mary pray for us and obtain grace and favours? Obviously, we can’t go up to heaven to find out! One thing we do know, however, is that Mary, our mother, wants only the best for us. Mary ardently wants us to have what God wants to give us, and she repeats this wish in her prayer. Her “intentions” are the same as those of God and this is why her prayers are always answered.

The mother is so intimately united to her Son that they cannot but love us in the same way and want for us only what is best. In short, the prayer of Mary is: “May your will be done on earth as in heaven” (Matthew 6:10). The Spirit of God still prays in her as during the time of her earthly life. In the “same action,” one might say, God inspires *and* answers Mary’s prayer.

Sometimes our imagination and our feelings can play tricks on us! For example, it is wrong to think that Mary must “inform” God about us, as though God were not up-to-date on our needs. Neither does she have to ask God to “pay attention to us,” as if God were indifferent to our life.

The God to whom Mary prays on our behalf is the same God who so loved the world "that he gave his only Son...so that through him the world might be saved" (John 3:16-17). It is through her, Mary, that God gave us his only Son. Today, it is still by this same woman, by her "yes" and her prayer, that God continues to give us his Son "full of grace and truth."

We were created for heaven, but the devil burned the ladder by which one could enter. Our Lord, by his passion, has made us another one... The Most Holy Virgin is at the top of the ladder holding it with her two hands...

St. John Vianney

Our Faith Is Great

“Our faith is great, when we think about it as we should.” This reflection of a friend comes back to my mind in ending this book. Yes, “our faith is great!” It is as great as the heart of God and as God’s work of love for us. Even before the creation of the world, while looking upon the Son, God thought of us. God chose us so that we could be in his love, holy and irreproachable before him. From the beginning we were destined to be God’s children through Jesus Christ.

When the time came, God sent the Son. He was born of a woman that we might become the sons and daughters of God (Galatians 4:4). Yes, it is through a woman that God has come. It is through a woman that God’s ‘dream to become like us so that we could become like him,” became a reality. “And the Virgin’s name was Mary” (Luke 1:27).

Glory to you, Lord,
for your humble servant!
The one whom you made so beautiful,
in your pure image and likeness.

You have chosen her
to accomplish great things in her.
Holy is your name!

Mary!
Happy mother in the midst of your children:
all together, the small and the great,
we proclaim you blessed.

We love you, Mary!

We, brothers and sisters of Jesus,
today and tomorrow and always,
with the angel, say to you:
"Rejoice!

The Lord is with thee!"

QUIZZES

Test your memory and knowledge, and have fun with the quizzes on the following pages. You can find the correct answers, beginning on page 171

CHAPTER 1

A. CHECK THE CORRECT ANSWER

1) *We call him the "father of believers" because he was the first to place his trust in the promise of God*
    a) ____ Adam
    b) ____ Abraham
    c) ____ Noah

2) *Mary's name in the language of her country*
    a) ____ Rachel
    b) ____ Rebecca
    c) ____ Miriam

3) *God chose Israel*
    a) ____ because of its military strength
    b) ____ because it deserved it
    c) ____ freely, through love

4) *The city where Mary lived*
    a) ____ Jerusalem
    b) ____ Nazareth
    c) ____ Cana

5) *He guided the Hebrew people in the desert*
   a) ____ David
   b) ____ Jacob
   c) ____ Moses

B. INDICATE WHETHER THE FOLLOWING SENTENCES ARE TRUE OR FALSE

1) *The Easter celebration signifies "passover."*
   ______ true
   ______ false

2) *The mother of Mary was named Elizabeth.*
   ______ true
   ______ false

3) *The Romans occupied Palestine in the time of Mary.*
   ______ true
   ______ false

4) *An apocryphal writing is a book of the Bible which recounts the childhood of Mary.*
   ______ true
   ______ false

5) *Mary was conceived in a miraculous way.*
   ______ true
   ______ false

C. COMPLETE THE FOLLOWING SENTENCES BY WRITING IN THE MISSING WORD(S)

1) At Sinai, God made a .... with the people.

2) God sent .... to the people to invite them to be faithful and to trust in God.

3) The Bible refers to the people who put their trust in God as ....

4) Mary eagerly awaited the .... whom God had promised.

5) The best known of the apocryphal writings is the ....

CHAPTER 2

A. CHECK THE CORRECT ANSWER

1) *"Immaculate Conception" means that Mary*
   a) ____ became a mother and remained a virgin
   b) ____ was preserved from sin and was filled with the love of God from the beginning of her existence in the womb of her mother
   c) ____ never sinned

2) *We became children of God and members of God's family*
   a) ____ at our Confirmation
   b) ____ at our Baptism
   c) ____ at our conception

3) *When we say "filled with grace," the word grace means*
   a) ____ the freely given favour of God
   b) ____ the merit of Mary
   c) ____ the purity of Mary

4) *Mary was preserved from original sin*
   a) ____ in view of the good deeds that she would carry out in her life
   b) ____ because her mother was holy
   c) ____ in view of the merits of Jesus Christ

5) *Sin is*
   a) ____ saying no to, and separating ourselves from, God
   b) ____ a weakness of character
   c) ____ a complex

B. INDICATE WHETHER THE FOLLOWING SENTENCES ARE TRUE OR FALSE

1) *God wants all people to be saved.*
   ______ true
   ______ false

2) *God loves little children in their mother's womb.*
   ______ true
   ______ false

3) *The Blessed Virgin did not need to be saved since she had never sinned.*
   ______ true
   ______ false

4) *God created the first humans with original sin.*
   ______ true
   ______ false

5) *God preserved Mary from sin in order to make her a mother worthy of the Son.*
   ______ true
   ______ false

C. COMPLETE THE FOLLOWING SENTENCES BY WRITING IN THE MISSING WORD(S)

1) We were all created in the image and .... of God.

2) The Immaculate Conception means that Mary was preserved from .... sin and was filled with the grace of God from the beginning of her existence.

3) All grace comes to us through ....

4) God was the .... to love us.

5) The pope who defined the dogma of the Immaculate Conception of Mary was ....

CHAPTER 3

A. CHECK THE RIGHT ANSWER

1) *The angel who brought the message to Mary was*
   a) ____ Raphael
   b) ____ Gabriel
   c) ____ Michael

2) *The mystery of God becoming human is called*
   a) ____ the Incarnation
   b) ____ the Redemption
   c) ____ the Creation

3) *The evangelist who recorded the announcement to Joseph was*
   a) ____ John
   b) ____ Luke
   c) ____ Matthew

4) *Mary is the mother of God because*
   a) ____ she existed before God
   b) ____ her Son is God
   c) ____ she is holy

5) *By saying she was the "servant" of the Lord, Mary affirmed that she is*
   a) ____ a member of the cleaning staff
   b) ____ at the service of the will of God
   c) ____ a domestic

B. INDICATE WHETHER THE FOLLOWING SENTENCES ARE TRUE OR FALSE

1) *Mary welcomed the Saviour in the name of all humanity.*
   ______ true
   ______ false

2) *Because she was immaculate in her conception, Mary knew in advance what was going to happen to her.*
   ______ true
   ______ false

3) *Jesus is not a human being since he is the Son of God.*
   ______ true
   ______ false

4) *Mary became pregnant because she was not given any choice. God forced her to say yes.*
   ______ true
   ______ false

5) *The Virgin Mary gave birth to Jesus without having sexual relations with Joseph.*
   ______ true
   ______ false

C. COMPLETE THE FOLLOWING SENTENCES BY WRITING IN THE MISSING WORD(S)

1) It is on Mary's .... that God made the divine coming into the world depend.

2) Mary answered: "I am the .... of the Lord. Be it done to me according to your ...."

3) The Virgin became pregnant with Jesus by the action of the ....

4) The Son of Mary is the Son of God, the Second .... of the Trinity.

5) In the *Creed*, we say: "I believe in God, the Father almighty, ... I believe in Jesus Christ, his only Son, our Lord. He was conceived by the power of .... and born of ....

CHAPTER 4

A. CHECK THE CORRECT ANSWER

1) *The first words of the angel Gabriel to Mary were:*
   a) ____ Remember
   b) ____ Rejoice
   c) ____ Do not be afraid

2) *The name of Elizabeth's baby was*
   a) ____ Jonathan
   b) ____ Daniel
   c) ____ John

3) *Elizabeth recognized the Lord in the unborn child that Mary carried because*
   a) ____ Mary had already informed her
   b) ____ she was filled with the Holy Spirit
   c) ____ Zechariah had heard it from the angel

4) *Elizabeth's small child "leaped" in her womb because of*
   a) ____ joy
   b) ____ nervousness
   c) ____ colic

5) *The words from the Bible: "Shout for joy, daughter of Zion... Rejoice, exult with all your heart... Yahweh your God is in your midst..." are from the book of*

a) ____ Isaiah
b) ____ Zephaniah
c) ____ Ezekiel

B. INDICATE WHETHER THE FOLLOWING SENTENCES ARE TRUE OR FALSE

1) *Mary went to visit Judith, her elderly cousin.*

______ true
______ false

2) *The Magnificat is a song of recognition to Mary.*

______ true
______ false

3) *Mary spent three days at her cousin's home.*

______ true
______ false

4) *Mary's cousin was married to Zechariah*

______ true
______ false

5) *During Mary's visit with Elizabeth, Joseph stayed at home to take care of the child Jesus.*

______ true
______ false

C. COMPLETE THESE SENTENCES BY WRITING IN THE MISSING WORD(S)

1) The Annunciation is the .... joyful mystery of the rosary.

2) Elizabeth was pregnant for .... months when Mary learned the news.

3) ''Humility is ....''

4) Mary prophesied: ''All generations shall call me ....''

5) The Gospel account of the Visitation mentions five "people." They are: ....

CHAPTER 5

A. INDICATE THE CORRECT ANSWERS

1) *Through Joseph, his adoptive father, Jesus was known as the descendant of*
   a) ____ Moses
   b) ____ David
   c) ____ Saul

2) *The father-in-law of Joseph is*
   a) ____ Zechariah
   b) ____ David
   c) ____ Joachim

3) *The synagogue was*
   a) ____ a market
   b) ____ a house of prayer
   c) ____ a fortress

4) *The "brothers" of Jesus mentioned in the Gospels may in fact be*
   a) ____ cousins or second cousins of Jesus
   b) ____ other children of Mary
   c) ____ friends of the family

5) *Joseph is often depicted with a lily in his hand to remind us*

a) ____ that he loved flowers
b) ____ that he lived a chaste life with Mary
c) ____ that this flower was the emblem of his family

B. INDICATE WHETHER THE FOLLOWING SENTENCES ARE TRUE OR FALSE

1) *Mary and Joseph lived as brother and sister.*

______ true
______ false

2) *According to the Jewish tradition, genealogies followed the woman's side of the family.*

___true
___false

3) *Engagement took place at an older age in Palestine.*

______ true
______ false

4) *Mary had many more children in addition to Jesus.*

______ true
______ false

5) *The lesson of Nazareth is that we are children of God in everything we do, whether big or small.*

______ true
______ false

C. COMPLETE THE FOLLOWING SENTENCES BY WRITING IN THE MISSING WORD(S)

1) The people of Nazareth accepted Jesus as the son of ....

2) In Mary's country, the age of majority for girls was ....

3) Mary was .... to Joseph when she became pregnant with Jesus.

4) If Joseph had been too old to father children when he married Mary, Mary could have been labelled an .... by the people.

5) The members of the Holy Family were ....

CHAPTER 6

A. CHECK THE CORRECT ANSWER

1) *Elizabeth congratulated Mary for*
   a) ____ her beauty
   b) ____ her faith
   c) ____ her marriage to Joseph

2) *Mary believed*
   a) ____ because she understood everything God had said
   b) ____ because she was sure of the Word of God
   c) ____ because everyone believed

3) *At Cana, Mary told the servants at the wedding:*
   a) ____ "They have no more wine."
   b) ____ "How can this be done?"
   c) ____ "Do whatever he tells you."

4) *Mary was great, and she was close to Jesus, because of*
   a) ____ her Immaculate Conception
   b) ____ her virginal maternity
   c) ____ her faith

5) *What Gospel tells us about the Annunciation to Mary and her Visitation to Elizabeth?*
   a) ____ Luke
   b) ____ John
   c) ____ Mark

B. INDICATE WHETHER THE FOLLOWING SENTENCES ARE TRUE OR FALSE

1) *Some of Jesus's relatives did not believe in him.*
   ______ true
   ______ false

2) *Mary believed in Jesus after the miracle at Cana.*
   ______ true
   ______ false

3) *Towards the end of Mary's pregnancy, King Herod ordered a census.*
   ______ true
   ______ false

4) *For Mary, it was easy to believe since she was with Jesus.*
   ______ true
   ______ false

5) *After Pentecost, Mary was able to meet Jesus in the Church exactly as we do today.*
   ______ true
   ______ false

C. COMPLETE THE FOLLOWING SENTENCES BY WRITING IN THE MISSING WORD(S)

1) In Bethlehem, Mary put her baby to bed in a ....

2) When Jesus was found again in the temple, he said to his mother: "Why did you look for me? Did you not know that I had to be in my ....?

3) Jesus said: "Anyone who .... of God, that person is my brother and sister and mother."

4) The angel had told her, and Mary was totally convinced that: "Nothing is .... to God."

5) At Easter, Jesus overcame our three most serious enemies: ....

CHAPTER 7

A. CHECK THE CORRECT ANSWER

1) *When the Gospel speaks of another life, it means*
   a) ____ reincarnation
   b) ____ an existence with extra-terrestrial beings
   c) ____ eternal life with God

2) *The mystery of the Assumption is a mystery of the rosary. It is the*
   a) ____ fourth joyful mystery
   b) ____ fourth glorious mystery
   c) ____ second glorious mystery

3) *The Assumption of Mary shows that the full realization of our life*
   a) ____ is found with God
   b) ____ depends on our capacity alone
   c) ____ is the result of chance and destiny

4) *The dogma of the Assumption was defined on November 1, 1950 by*
   a) ____ John the Twenty-Third
   b) ____ Paul the Sixth
   c) ____ Pius the Twelfth

5) *We celebrate the Assumption of Mary on*
   a) ____ August 15
   b) ____ December 8
   c) ____ March 25

B. INDICATE WHETHER THE FOLLOWING SENTENCES ARE TRUE OR FALSE

1) *In the end, Jesus will raise us all together.*
   ______ true
   ______ false

2) *Mary is the "first of the saved."*
   ______ true
   ______ false

3) *It is possible to be a disciple of Jesus and to believe in the reincarnation at the same time.*
   ______ true
   ______ false

4) *Since the Resurrection, Jesus can be everywhere at the same time.*
   ______ true
   ______ false

5) *Because Mary is the mother of Jesus, she has her own personal heaven.*
   ______ true
   ______ false

C. COMPLETE THE FOLLOWING SENTENCES BY WRITING IN THE THE MISSING WORD(S)

1) On the day of the ...., Mary entered, body and soul, into eternal life.

2) As with Jesus, God will also give life to our mortal bodies through the .... which dwells in us.

3) We will be .... God because we will see him as he is.

4) Those who .... their life for Jesus and the Gospel will .... for life eternal.

5) Those who believe in .... say that our body is not part of our person, but is only an envelope, a shell for our spirit.

CHAPTER 8

A. CHECK THE CORRECT ANSWER

1) *"This is your son, this is your mother." We can find these words in the Gospel of John at*
   a) ____ chapter 11, verse 25
   b) ____ chapter 10, verse 11
   c) ____ chapter 19, verse 26

2) *While speaking of the "let it be" of Mary at Calvary, we recall*
   a) ____ that she consented to the sacrifice of Jesus
   b) ____ that she cried
   c) ____ that she was nearby

3) *Mary is the mother*
   a) ____ of all human beings
   b) ____ of Christians only
   c) ____ of those who know her

4) *When Jesus spoke of his "hour," he was thinking of*
   a) ____ the multiplication of the loaves of bread
   b) ____ Calvary
   c) ____ the Transfiguration

5) *The mother of the Church is*
   a) ____ above the Church
   b) ____ outside the Church
   c) ____ in the Church

B. INDICATE WHETHER THE FOLLOWING SENTENCES ARE TRUE OR FALSE

1) *The Virgin Mary is the first disciple of Jesus.*
   ______ true
   ______ false

2) *The mother of Jesus is our sister since she, too, is a member of the human race.*
   ______ true
   ______ false

3) *Jesus did not want his mother to see him die, so he sent her back to Nazareth.*
   ______ true
   ______ false

4) *Mary agreed that Jesus should give of himself completely, even to giving up his life for his people.*
   ______ true
   ______ false

5) *After Jesus's death, Mary went to live with the apostle Peter.*
   ______ true
   ______ false

C. COMPLETE THE FOLLOWING SENTENCES BY WRITING IN THE MISSING WORD(S)

1) Jesus said: "I have come so that people might have .... in abundance."

2) The .... is the "family" of the disciples of Jesus.

3) At Cana, Jesus said to his mother: "Woman, my .... has not yet ...."

4) Jesus died to .... the scattered children of God.

5) On Calvary, the prophecy of .... was realized for Mary: "Your heart will be pierced with a sword."

CHAPTER 9

A. CHECK THE CORRECT ANSWER

1) *"Jesus is always living and prays (interecedes) on our behalf." These words can be found in*
   a) ____ Hebrews 2:11
   b) ____ Hebrews 12:2
   c) ____ Hebrews 7:25

2) *The expression "communion of saints"*
   a) ____ refers to the fervour of the saints when they receive communion
   b) ____ signifies the sharing, the deep union that exists between the members of the Church
   c) ____ refers to the liturgical calendar

3) When Mary prays to God for us
   a) ____ she tells God about our needs
   b) ____ she appeases God's anger against us
   c) ____ her intentions are the same as those of God

4) *Mary is merciful and good because*
   a) ____ of her good temperament
   b) ____ God made her able to love as God does
   c) ____ she imagines us to be better than we are

5) *The risen Jesus has entered into heaven*
   a) ____ with his body and soul
   b) ____ with his soul only
   c) ____ by ceasing to be a human being

B. INDICATE WHETHER THE FOLLOWING SENTENCES ARE TRUE OR FALSE

1) *The Virgin Mary makes a "bridge" between Jesus and us."*
   ______ true
   ______ false

2) *Because Mary is our mother, she understands us better than God does.*
   ______ true
   ______ false

3) *Our brothers and sisters in heaven are no longer part of the Church since they are with God.*
   ______ true
   ______ false

4) *Jesus is the mediator of all graces.*
   ______ true
   ______ false

5) *The communion of saints is part of the Catholic faith.*
   ______ true
   ______ false

C. COMPLETE THE FOLLOWING SENTENCES BY WRITING IN THE CORRECT WORD(S)

1) .... prophesied: ''I will spend .... doing good on earth.''

2) The closer we are to God, the .... we are to one another.

3) ''God so .... the world that he .... his only Son so that the world may be .... by him.''

4) In the Church, the person who can help us the most is ....

5) Everything passes through Jesus. That is why we say in the Mass: "........................ him, ... him, and .... him, in the unity .... all glory and honour are yours."

ANSWERS TO THE QUIZZES

CHAPTER 1

A.
1) b. 2) c. 3) c. 4) b. 5) c.

B.
1) true. 2) false, she was called Anne. 3) true. 4) false, an apocryphal writing is not a book of the Bible. 5) false, she was conceived like other children.

C.
1) covenant (alliance). 2) prophets. 3) poor (humble, right hearted). 4) Messiah. 5) Protogospel of James.

CHAPTER 2

A.
1) b. 2) b. 3) a. 4) c. 5) a.

B.
1) true. 2) true. 3) false, it is true that she never sinned, but she had to be saved from original sin. 4) false, God created the first humans in his friendship (state of grace). 5) true.

C.
1) his likeness. 2) original. 3) Jesus. 4) first. 5) Pius the Ninth.

CHAPTER 3

A.
1) b. 2) a. 3) c. 4) b. 5) b.

B.
1) true. 2) false, Mary did not know in advance. 3) false, Jesus is the Son of God, but he is also a human being. 4) false, she accepted it freely. 5) true.

C.
1) yes (consent). 2) servant... word. 3) Holy Spirit. 4) Person. 5) Creator of heaven and earth... the Holy Spirit ...the Virgin Mary.

CHAPTER 4

A.
1) b. 2) c. 3) b. 4) a. 5) b.

B.
1) false, her cousin was called Elizabeth. 2) false, it is a song to God. 3) false, she was there three months. 4) true. 5) false, Mary was pregnant with Jesus.

C.
1) first. 2) six. 3) truth. 4) blessed. 5) Mary, Elizabeth, Jesus, John and the Holy Spirit.

CHAPTER 5

A.
1) b. 2) c. 3) b. 4) a. 5) b.

B.
1) true. 2) false, it follows the man's side of the family. 3) false, they were engaged very young. 4) false. 5) true.

C.
1) Joseph. 2) twelve and a half years. 3) engaged (betrothed). 4) adulteress. 5) Jesus, Mary, Joseph.

CHAPTER 6

A.
1) b. 2) b. 3) c. 4) c. 5) a.

B.
1) true. 2) false, she already believed before the miracle of Cana. 3) false, it was the Roman emperor who ordered the census. 4) false, for Mary it was not easy to believe. She was sometimes "unsettled" by the words and actions of Jesus. 5) true.

C.
1) manger. 2) Father's house. 3) does the will. 4) impossible. 5) Satan, sin, death.

CHAPTER 7

A.
1) c. 2) b. 3) a. 4) c. 5) a.

B.
1) true. 2) true. 3) false, believing in reincarnation and being a disciple of Jesus are contradictory. 4) true. 5) false, to be in heaven is to be with God, so there are not several heavens.

C.
1) Assumption. 2) Spirit. 3) like (in the likeness). 4) lose... save it. 5) reincarnation.

CHAPTER 8

A.
1) c. 2) a. 3) a. 4) b. 5) c.

B.
1) true. 2) true. 3) false, Mary was present at the death of Jesus. 4) true. 5) false, she went to live with John.

C.
1) life. 2) Church. 3) hour... come. 4) gather. 5) Simeon.

CHAPTER 9

A.

1) c. 2) b. 3) c. 4) b. 5) a.

B.

1) false, we are directly united with Jesus, we do not need a bridge to make contact with him. 2) false, God understands us. God is Love. 3) false, our brothers and sisters in heaven are also part of the Church. 4) true. 5) true.

C.

1) Saint Theresa of the Child Jesus… my heaven. 2) closer. 3) loved… gave… saved. 4) Mary. 5) through… with… in… of the Holy Spirit

ALPHABETICAL TABLE